Abu Ghraib

Abu Ghraib
The Politics of Torture

With Essays by
>Meron Benvenisti, Mark Danner,
>Barbara Ehrenreich, John Gray,
>Richard Grossinger, David Matlin,
>Charles Stein, David Levi Strauss,
>and Brooke Warner

THE TERRA NOVA SERIES
North Atlantic Books
Berkeley • California

Published by
North Atlantic Books
P.O. Box 12327
Berkeley, California 94712

Cover and book design by Paula Morrison
Printed in the United States of America
Distributed to the book trade by Publishers Group West

Abu Ghraib: The Politics of Torture is sponsored by the Society for the Study of Native Arts and Sciences, a nonprofit educational corporation whose goals are to develop an educational and crosscultural perspective linking various scientific, social, and artistic fields; to nurture a holistic view of arts, sciences, humanities, and healing; and to publish and distribute literature on the relationship of mind, body, and nature.

Library of Congress Cataloging-in-Publication Data

Abu Ghraib : the politics of torture / with essays by Meron Benvenisti, Mark Danner, Barbara Ehrenreich, John Gray, Richard Grossinger, David Matlin, Charles Stein, David Levi Strauss, and Brooke Warner.

     p. cm. — (The Terra nova series)

  ISBN 1-55643-550-9 (pbk.)

  1. Iraq War, 2003—Prisoners and prisons, Americans. 2. Iraq War, 2003—Atrocities. 3. Torture—Iraq. 4. Political prisoners—Iraq. 5. Abu Graib Prison. I. Benvenisti, Meron, 1934– II. Series.

  DS79.76.A28 2004

  956.7044'31—dc22

2004020384

1 2 3 4 5 6 7 8 9 DATA 09 08 07 06 05 04

Table of Contents

Permissions

George Bush the younger arrives at St. Peter's Gate. St. Peter greets him and then throws out an unexpected question: "Would you rather go to heaven or hell?" W. looks puzzled. He didn't realize he had a choice—and isn't the choice obvious? In fact, he is tongue-tied.

"I'll tell you what I'll do for you," St. Peter says; "I'll give you a day in each place and then you can decide."

W. takes him up on the offer.

The first day is in hell. W. is amazed. It may be a bit stark, but it's not bad at all. Many of his friends are there: Cheney, Rummy, Ken Lay, Prince Bander. . . . He has a wonderful time reminiscing with each of them. Then he is returned to St. Peter.

The next day the gatekeeper places him in heaven.

There is no denying heaven is a beautiful place, a true paradise. But W. is bored. He sees no one he knows, and scenery doesn't amount to much in the absence of fellowship. He wanders around for a day before he finds himself back at the pearly gate.

To his own astonishment, he chooses hell.

On his arrival back below he sees devils roasting screaming people on spits, fires spouting everywhere. "But it wasn't like this before!" he screams.

Glancing up, one of the devils says, "That was the campaign. This is the real thing."

viii

1.
Torture and Truth

Mark Danner

Last November in Iraq, I traveled to Fallujah during the early days of what would become known as the "Ramadan Offensive"—when suicide bombers in the space of less than an hour destroyed the Red Cross headquarters and four police stations, and daily attacks by insurgents against U.S. troops doubled, and the American adventure in Iraq entered a bleak tunnel from which it has yet to emerge. I inquired of a young man there why the people of that city were attacking Americans more frequently each day. How many of the attacks, I wanted to know, were carried out by foreign fighters? How many by local Islamists? And how many by what U.S. officers called "FRL's"—former regime loyalists?[1]

The young man—I'll call him Salih—listened, answered patiently in his limited but eloquent English, but soon became impatient with what he plainly saw as my American obsession with categories and particulars. Finally he interrupted my litany of questions, pushed his face close to mine, and spoke to me slowly and emphatically:

For Fallujans it is a *shame* to have foreigners break down their doors. It is a *shame* for them to have foreigners stop and search their women. It is a *shame* for the foreigners to put a bag over their heads, to make a man lie on the ground with your shoe on his neck. This is a great *shame,* you understand? This is a great *shame* for the whole tribe.

It is the *duty* of that man, and of that tribe, to get revenge on this soldier—to kill that man. Their duty is to attack them, to *wash the shame.* The shame is a *stain,* a dirty thing; they have to *wash* it. No sleep— we cannot sleep until we have revenge. They have to kill soldiers.

He leaned back and looked at me, then tried one more time. "The Americans," he said, "*provoke* the people. They don't *respect* the people."

I thought of Salih and his impatience as I paged through the reports of General Taguba and the Red Cross,[2] for they treat not just of "abuses" or "atrocities" but the entire American "liberation" of Iraq and how it has gone wrong; they are dispatches from the scene of a political disaster. Salih came strongly to mind as I read one of the less lurid sections of the Red Cross report, entitled "Treatment During Arrest," in which the anonymous authors tell how Iraqis they'd interviewed described "a fairly consistent pattern . . . of brutality by members of the [Coalition Forces] arresting them:"

Arresting authorities entered houses usually after dark, breaking down doors, waking up residents roughly, yelling orders, forcing family members into one room under military guard while searching the rest of the house and further breaking doors, cabinets and other property. They arrested suspects, tying their hands in the back with flexi-cuffs, hooding them, and taking them away. Sometimes they arrested all adult males present in a house, including elderly, handicapped or sick people . . . pushing people around, insulting, taking aim with rifles, punching and kicking and striking with rifles.

Of course, this is war; those soldiers had intelligence to gather, insurgents to find, a rebellion to put down. However frightening such nighttime arrests might be, Iraqis could at least expect that these soldiers were accountable, that they had commanding officers and a clear chain of command, that there were bases to which one could go and complain. These were, after all, Americans. And yet:

In almost all instances, . . . arresting authorities provided no in formation about who they were, where

3

their base was located, nor did they explain the cause of arrest. Similarly, they rarely informed the arrestee or his family where he was being taken and for how long, resulting in the de facto "disappearance" of the arrestee.... Many [families] were left without news for months, often fearing that their relatives were dead.

We might pass over with a shiver the word "disappearance," with its unfortunate associations, and say to ourselves, once again, that this was war: insurgents were busy killing American soldiers and had to be rooted out, even if it meant one or two innocent civilians were sucked up into the system. And then one comes upon this quiet little sentence:

Certain [Coalition Forces] military intelligence officers told the ICRC that in their estimate between *70 percent and 90 percent of the persons deprived of their liberty in Iraq had been arrested by mistake.* [emphasis added]

Abu Ghraib contained within its walls last fall—as the war heated up and American soldiers, desperate for "actionable intelligence," spent many an autumn evening swooping down on Iraqi homes, kicking in doors, and carrying away hooded prisoners into the night—well over 8,000

4

Iraqis. Could it be that "between 70 percent and 90 percent" of them were "arrested by mistake?" And if so, which of the naked, twisted bodies that television viewers and newspaper readers around the world have been gazing at these last weeks were among them? Perhaps the seven bodies piled up in that great coil, buttocks and genitals exposed to the camera? Or the bodies bound one against another on the cellblock floor? Or the body up against the bars, clenched before the teeth of barking police dogs?

Consider the naked body wearing only the black hood, hands clasped above its head: Pfc. Lynndie England, she of the famous leash, frames the body like a car salesman displaying next year's model, grinning back at the camera, pointing to its genitals with her right hand, flashing a thumbs-up with her left. This body belongs to Hayder Sabbar Abd, a thirty-four-year-old Shiite from Nasi riya, also known as Abu Ghraib Prisoner Number 13077. Last June, at a military checkpoint in the south, according to *The New York Times,* Mr. Abd "tried to leave the taxi he was riding in." Suspicious behavior, rendered more suspicious by the fact that Mr. Abd had served eighteen years in the Iraqi army, part of that time in the Republican Guard. The Americans took him to a detention center at Baghdad airport, and from there to the big military prison at Um Qasr, and finally, after three months, to Abu Ghraib. A strange odyssey through Occupied Iraq, made stranger by the fact that during that time, Mr. Abd says, "he was never interrogated, and never charged with a crime." "The truth is," he told Ian Fisher of *The New York Times,* "we were not terrorists. We were not insurgents. We were just ordinary people. And American intelligence knew this."

As I write, we know nothing of what "American intelligence knew"—apart from a hint here or there, this critical fact is wholly absent from both reports, as it has been from the public hearings of Secretary of Defense Donald Rumsfeld and other officials. General Taguba, following his orders, concentrates instead on the activities of the military police, hapless amateurs who were "tasked" to "set physical and mental conditions for favorable interrogation of witnesses" and whose work, thanks to digital photography, has now been displayed so vividly to the citizens of the world. It is this photography that has let us visualize something of what happened to Mr. Abd one night in early November, following a fight among prisoners, when he and six other men were brought to what was known as "the hard site" at Abu Ghraib, the wing for the most dangerous prisoners:

The seven men were all placed in hoods, he said, and the beating began. "They beat our heads on the walls and the doors," he said. "I don't really know: I couldn't see." He said his jaw had been broken, badly enough that he still has trouble eating. In all, he said, he believes that he received about fifty blows over about two hours.

"Then the interpreter told us to strip," he said. "We told him: 'You are Egyptian, and you are a Muslim. You know that as Muslims we can't do that.' When we refused to take off our clothes, they beat us and tore our clothes off with a blade."

It was at this moment in the interview . . . that several pages of the photographs made public last week were produced. . . . He quickly and unemotionally pointed out all his friends—Hussein, Ah med, Hashim—naked, hooded, twisted around each other.

He also saw himself, as degraded as possible: naked, his hand on his genitals, a female soldier, identified in another report as Pfc. Lynndie England, pointing and smiling with a cigarette in her mouth. Mr. Abd said one of the soldiers had removed his hood, and the translator ordered him to masturbate while looking at Private England. . . .

"She was laughing, and she put her hands on her breasts," Mr. Abd said. "Of course, I couldn't do it. I told them that I couldn't, so they beat me in the stomach, and I fell to the ground. The translator said, 'Do it! Do it! It's better than being beaten.' I said, 'How can I do it?' So I put my hand on my penis, just pretending."

All the while, he said, the flash of the camera kept illuminating the dim room that once held prisoners of Mr. Hussein. . . . [3]

Such scenes, President Bush tells us, "do not represent America." But for Iraqis, what does? To Salih and other Iraqis they represent the logical extension of treatment they have seen every day under a military occupation that began harshly and has grown, under the stress of the insurgency, more brutal. As another young Iraqi man told me in November,

The attacks on the soldiers have made the army close down. You go outside and there's a guy on a Humvee pointing a machine gun at you. You learn to raise your hands, to turn around. You come to hate the Americans.

This of course is a prime goal of the insurgents; they cannot defeat the Americans militarily but they can defeat them politically. For the insurgents, the path to such victory lies in provoking the American occupiers to do their political work for them; the insurgents ambush American convoys with "improvised explosive devices" placed in city neighborhoods so the Americans will respond by wounding and killing civilians, or by imprisoning them in places like Abu Ghraib.[4] The insurgents want to place the outnumbered, overworked American troops under constant fear and stress so they will mistreat Iraqis on a broad scale and succeed in making themselves hated.

In this project, as these reports make clear, the methods used at Abu Ghraib played a critical part. For if Americans are learning about these "abuses" for the first time, news about what has been happening at Abu Ghraib and other prisons has been spreading throughout Iraq for many months. And if the Iraqis, with their extensive experience of Abu Ghraib and the purposes it served in the national imagination, do not regard such methods as "abuses," neither do the investigators of the Red Cross:

> These methods of physical and psychological coercion *were used by the military intelligence in a systematic way to gain confessions and extract information* or other forms of co-operation from persons who had been arrested in connection with suspected security offences or deemed to have an "intelligence value." [emphasis added]

What, according to the Red Cross, were these "methods of physical and psychological coercion"?

• Hooding, used to prevent people from seeing and to disorient them, and also to prevent them from breathing freely. One or sometimes two bags, sometimes with an elastic blindfold over the eyes which, when slipped down, further impeded proper breathing. Hooding was sometimes used in conjunction with beatings thus increasing anxiety as to when blows would come. The practice of hooding also allowed the interrogators to remain anonymous and thus to act with impunity. Hooding could last for periods from a few hours to up to two to four consecutive days . . . ;

• Handcuffing with flexi-cuffs, which were sometimes made so tight and used for such extended periods that they caused skin lesions and long-term after-effects on the hands (nerve damage), as observed by the ICRC;

• Beatings with hard objects (including pistols and rifles), slapping, punching, kicking with knees or feet on various parts of the body (legs, sides, lower back, groin) . . . ;

• Being paraded naked outside cells in front of other persons deprived of their liberty, and guards, sometimes hooded or with women's underwear over the head . . . ;

• Being attached repeatedly over several days . . . with handcuffs to the bars of their cell door in humiliating (i.e. naked or in underwear) and/or uncomfortable position causing physical pain;

• Exposure while hooded to loud noise or music, prolonged exposure while hooded to the sun over several hours, including during the hottest time of the day when temperatures could reach ... 122 degrees Fahrenheit ... or higher;

• Being forced to remain for prolonged periods in stress positions such as squatting or standing with or without the arms lifted.

The authors of the Red Cross report note that when they visited the "isolation section" of Abu Ghraib in mid-October 2003, they "directly witnessed and documented a variety of methods used to secure the cooperation" of prisoners, among them "the practice of keeping [prisoners] completely naked in totally empty concrete cells and in total darkness...." When the Red Cross delegates "requested an explanation from the authorities ... the military intelligence officer in charge of the interrogation explained that this practice was 'part of the process.'"

The ICRC medical delegate examined persons ... presenting signs of concentration difficulties, memory problems, verbal expression difficulties, incoherent speech, acute anxiety reactions, abnormal behavior and suicidal tendencies. These symptoms appeared to have been caused by the methods and duration of interrogation.

This "process" is not new; indeed, like so many of the news stories presented as "revelation" during these last few months, it has appeared before in the American press. After the arrest in Pakistan more than a year ago of Khalid Sheik Mohammed, the al-Qaeda operations chief, "senior American officials" told *The New York Times* that "physical torture would not be used against Mr. Mohammed":

> They said his interrogation would rely on what they consider acceptable techniques like sleep and light deprivation and the temporary withholding of food, water, access to sunlight and medical attention.

American officials acknowledged that such techniques were recently applied as part of the interrogation of Abu Zubaydah, the highest-ranking Qaeda operative in custody until the capture of Mr. Mohammed. Painkillers were withheld from Mr. Zubaydah, who was shot several times during his capture in Pakistan.[5]

In the same article, published more than a year ago, a number of American officials discussed the "methods and techniques" applied in interrogations at Afghanistan's Bagram Air Base, at Guantanamo, and at other secret prisons now holding the thousands who have been arrested and confined by American and allied forces since the attacks of September 11:

Routine techniques include covering suspects' heads with black hoods for hours at a time and forcing them to stand or kneel in uncomfortable positions in extreme cold or heat. . . . In some cases, American officials said, women are used as interrogators to try to humiliate men. . . .

Disorientation is a tool of interrogation and therefore a way of life. To that end, the building—an unremarkable hangar—is lighted twenty-four hours a day, making sleep almost impossible, said Muhammad Shah, an Afghan farmer who was held there for eighteen days.

Colonel King said it was legitimate to use lights, noise and vision restriction, and to alter, without warning, the time between meals, to blur a detainee's sense of time. He said sleep deprivation was "probably within the lexicon. . . ."

Two former prisoners said they had been forced to stand with their hands chained to the ceiling and their feet shackled in the isolation cells.

The "methods of physical and psychological coercion" that the Red Cross delegates witnessed at Abu Ghraib were indeed, as the "military intelligence officer in charge of the interrogation" told them frankly, "part of" a "process" that has been deployed by American interrogators in the various

American-run secret prisons throughout the world since September 11. What separates Abu Ghraib from the rest is not the "methods of physical and psychological coercion used" but the fact that, under the increasing stress of the war, the pressing need for intelligence, and the shortage of available troops and other resources in Iraq, military policemen like Pfc. England, who had little or no training, were pressed into service to "soften up" the prisoners and, as the Taguba report puts it, set "the conditions for successful exploitation of the internees." And so when Specialist Sabrina Harman was asked about the prisoner who was placed on a box with electric wires attached to his fingers, toes, and penis, in an image now famous throughout the world, she replied that "her job was to keep detainees awake," that "MI [military intelligence] wanted to get them to talk," and that it was the job of her and her colleagues "to do things for MI and OGA [Other Government Agencies, a euphemism for the CIA] to get these people to talk." The military police, who, General Taguba notes, had "no training in interrogation," were told, in the words of Sergeant Javal S. Davis, to "loosen this guy up for us." "Make sure he has a bad night." "Make sure he gets the treatment."

As for the unusual methods used—"breaking of chemical lights and pouring the phosphoric liquid on detainees," "using military working dogs to frighten and intimidate detainees," "beating detainees with a broom handle and a chair," "threatening male detainees with rape," "sodomizing a detainee with a chemical light and perhaps a broom stick," and the rest of the sad litany General Taguba patiently sets out—Sergeant Davis told investigators that he "assumed that if they were doing things out of the ordinary or outside the guidelines, someone would have said something. Also the wing belongs to MI and it appeared MI personnel approved of the abuse."

Many of the young Americans smiling back at us in the photographs will soon be on trial. It is unlikely that those who ran "the process" and issued the orders will face the same tribunals. Iraqis will be well aware of this, even if Americans are not. The question is whether Americans have traveled far enough from the events of September 11 to go beyond the photographs, which show nothing more than the amateur stooges of "the process," and look squarely at the process itself, the process that goes on daily at Abu Ghraib, Guantanamo, Bagram, and other secret prisons in Iraq and around the world.

To date the true actors in those lurid scenes, who are professionals and no doubt embarrassed by the garish brutality of their apprentices in the military police, have remained offstage. None has testified. The question we must ask in coming days, as Specialist Jeremy Sivits and other young

Americans face public courts-martial in Baghdad, is whether or not we as Americans can face a true revelation. We must look squarely at the photographs and ask: Is what has changed only what we know, or what we are willing to accept?

—May 12, 2004
(This is the first of two articles.)

1. See my "Delusions in Baghdad," *The New York Review,* December 18, 2003.
2. *Article 15-6 Investigation of the 800th Military Police Brigade (The Taguba Report)*

   by Major General Antonio M. Taguba

   Report of the International Committee of the Red Cross (ICRC) on the Treatment by the Coalition Forces of Prisoners of War and Other Protected Persons by the Geneva Conventions in Iraq During Arrest, Internment and Interrogation

   by Delegates of the International Committee of the Red Cross, February 2004
3. See "Iraqi Recounts Hours of Abuse by US Troops," *The New York Times,* May 5, 2004, p. A1.
4. See my "Iraq: The New War," *The New York Review,* September 25, 2003.
5. See Don Van Natta Jr., "Questioning Terror Suspects in a Dark and Surreal World," *The New York Times,* March 9, 2003.

2.
The Logic of Torture

Mark Danner

1.

> We've now had fifteen of the highest-level officials
> involved in this entire operation, from the secretary
> of defense to the generals in command, and nobody
> knew that anything was amiss, no one approved any-
> thing amiss, nobody did anything amiss. We have a
> general acceptance of responsibility, but there's no
> one to blame, except for the people at the very bot-
> tom of one prison.
>
> —Senator Mark Dayton (D-Minn.),
> Armed Services Committee, May 19, 2004

What is difficult is separating what we now know from what
we have long known but have mostly refused to admit.
Though the events and disclosures of the last weeks have
taken on the familiar clothing of a Washington scandal—
complete with full-dress congressional hearings, daily leaks
to reporters from victim and accused alike, and of course
the garish, spectacular photographs and videos from Abu

Ghraib—beyond that bright glare of revelation lies a dark area of unacknowledged clarity. Behind the exotic brutality so painstakingly recorded in Abu Ghraib, and the multiple tangled plotlines that will be teased out in the coming weeks and months about responsibility, knowledge, and culpability, lies a simple truth, well known but not yet publicly admitted in Washington: that since the attacks of September 11, 2001, officials of the United States, at various locations around the world, from Bagram in Afghanistan to Guantanamo in Cuba to Abu Ghraib in Iraq, have been torturing prisoners. They did this, in the felicitous phrasing of General Taguba's report, in order to "exploit [them] for actionable intelligence" and they did it, insofar as this is possible, with the institutional approval of the United States government, complete with memoranda from the President's counsel and officially promulgated decisions, in the case of Afghanistan and Guantanamo, about the nonapplicability of the Geneva Conventions and, in the case of Iraq, about at least three different sets of interrogation policies, two of them modeled on earlier practice in Afghanistan and Cuba.[1]

They did it under the gaze of Red Cross investigators, whose confidential reports—which, after noting that "methods of physical and psychological coercion were used by the military intelligence in a systematic way to gain confessions and extract information," then set out these "methods" in stark and sickening detail[2]—were handed over to American military and government authorities and then mysteriously "became lost in the Army's bureaucracy and weren't adequately addressed."[3] Or so three of the highest-ranking military officers in the land blandly explained to senators on the Armed Services Committee on May 19. On that same day, as it happened, an unnamed "senior Army officer who served in Iraq" told reporters for *The New York Times* that in fact the Army *had* addressed the Red Cross report—"by trying to curtail the international organization's spot inspections of the prison:"

> After the International Committee of the Red Cross observed abuses in one cellblock on two unannounced inspections in October and complained in writing on November 6, the military responded that inspectors should make appointments before visiting the cellblock. That area was the site of the worst abuses.... Brig. Gen. Janis Karpinski, commander of the 800th Military Police Brigade, whose soldiers guarded the prisoners, said that despite the serious allegations in the Red Cross report, senior officers in Baghdad had treated it in "a light-hearted manner."[4]

Why had these "senior officers" treated the grave allegations of the Red Cross, now the subject of so much high-level attention, in "a lighthearted manner?" The most plausible answer is that they did so not because they were irresponsible or incompetent or evil but because they were well aware that this report—like the others that had been issued by the Red Cross, and by Amnesty International and Human Rights Watch and other well-known organizations—would have no bearing whatever on what the American military did or did not do in Iraq.

The officers almost certainly knew that, whatever the investigators of the Red Cross observed and wrote, American policies in Abu Ghraib prison were governed by entirely different concerns, and were sanctioned, even as the insurgency in Iraq gained strength and the demand for "actionable intelligence" became more urgent, by their most senior commanders—among others, by Lieutenant General Ricardo Sanchez, the overall commander in Iraq, who on October 12 (about the time Red Cross investigators were making their two unannounced inspections) signed a classified memorandum calling for interrogators at Abu Ghraib to work with military police guards to "manipulate an internee's emotions and weaknesses" and to assume control over the "lighting, heating ... food, clothing, and shelter" of those they were questioning.[5]

Six weeks later, Brigadier General Karpinski herself wrote to Red Cross officials to say that "military necessity" required the isolation of prisoners of "significant intelligence value" who were not, she asserted, entitled to "obtain full [Geneva Convention] protection," despite the Bush administration's stated position that the conventions would be "fully applicable" in Iraq.[6] We now have a good deal of evidence about how military policemen at Abu Ghraib, who had been ordered (according to Sergeant Samuel Provance, one of the first soldiers in military intelligence to speak to reporters) to "strip down prisoners and embarrass them as a way to help 'break' them,"[7] attempted, whether enthusiastically or reluctantly, to fulfill these orders.

2.

We can begin with the story of the as-yet-anonymous prisoner who on January 21, 2004, gave a sworn statement—obtained by *The Washington Post*—to the military's Criminal Investigation Division about his time in Abu Ghraib:

> The first day they put me in a dark room and started hitting me in the head and stomach and legs.
>
> They made me raise my hands and sit on my knees. I was like that for four hours. Then the Interrogator came and he was looking at me while they were beating

me. Then I stayed in this room for five days, naked with no clothes. . . . They put handcuffs on my hand and they cuffed me high for seven or eight hours. And that caused a rupture to my right hand and I had a cut that was bleeding and had pus coming from it. They kept me this way on 24, 25, and 26 October. And in the following days, they also put a bag over my head, and of course, this whole time I was without clothes and without anything to sleep on. And one day in November, they started different type of punishment, where an American Police came in my room and put the bag over my head and cuffed my hands and he took me out of the room into the hallway. He started beating me, him, and five other American Police. I could see their feet, only, from under the bag.

A couple of those police they were female because I heard their voices and I saw two of the police that were hitting me before they put the bag over my head. One of them was wearing glasses. I couldn't read his name because he put tape over his name. Some of the things they did was make me sit down like a dog, and they would hold the string from the bag and they made me bark like a dog and they were laughing at me. . . . One of the police was telling me to crawl in

Arabic, so I crawled on my stomach and the police were spitting on me when I was crawling and hitting me. . . .

Then the police started beating me on my kidneys and then they hit me on my right ear and it started bleeding and I lost consciousness. . . .

A few days before they hit me on my ear, the American police, the guy who wears glasses, he put red woman's underwear over my head. And then he tied me to the window that is in the cell with my hands behind my back until I lost consciousness. And also when I was in Room #1 they told me to lay down on my stomach and they were jumping from the bed onto my back and my legs. And the other two were spitting on me and calling me names, and they held my hands and legs. After the guy with the glasses got tired, two of the American soldiers brought me to the ground and tied my hands to the door while laying down on my stomach. One of the police was pissing on me and laughing on me. . . . And the soldier and his friend told me in a loud voice to lie down, so I did that. And then the policeman was opening my legs, with a bag over my head, and he sat down between my legs on his knees and I was looking at him from under the bag and they wanted to do me because I saw him and he was opening his pants, so I started screaming loudly and the other police starting hitting me with his feet on my neck and he put his feet on my head so I couldn't scream. . . . And then they put the loudspeaker inside the room and they closed the door and he was yelling in the microphone. . . .

They took me to the room and they signaled me to get on to the floor. And one of the police he put a part of his stick that he always carries inside my ass and I felt it going inside me about two centimeters, approximately. And I started screaming, and he pulled it out and he washed it with water inside the room. And then two American girls that were there when they were beating me, they were hitting me with a ball made of sponge on my dick. And when I was tied up in my room, one of the girls, with blonde hair, she is white, she was playing with my dick. . . . And they were taking pictures of me during all these instances.[8]

What is one to make of this Dantesque nightmare journey? The very outlandishness of the brutality might lead one to think such acts, if not themselves fantasies, must be the product of a singularly sadistic mind—and that indeed, as the Army has maintained, we are dealing here with the abuses of a half-dozen or so unstable personalities, left unsupervised, their natures darkened and corrupted by the stresses of war and homesickness and by the virtually unlimited power that had been granted them. That the abuse reported by many other Abu Ghraib detainees in their affidavits, and depicted in the photographs, is very similar does not of course disprove the Army's "few bad apples" defense; on the contrary, perhaps these half-dozen or so miscreants simply terrorized their cellblock, inflicting similar abhorrent acts on anyone they pleased. But then we come upon the following report, written by the Reuters bureau chief in Baghdad and published in the magazine *Editor and Publisher,* about the treatment of three Iraqi employees of Reuters—two cameramen and a driver—who were filming near the site of the downing of a U.S. helicopter near Fallujah in early January when troops of the 82nd Airborne Division arrived:

> When the soldiers approached them they were standing by their car, a blue Opel. Salem Uraiby [who had worked for Reuters as a cameraman for twelve years] shouted "Reuters, Reuters, journalist, journalist." At least one shot was fired into the ground close to them.
>
> They were thrown to the ground and soldiers placed guns to their heads. Their car was searched. Soldiers found their camera equipment and press badges and discovered no weapons of any kind. Their

hands were cuffed behind their backs and they were thrown roughly into a Humvee where they lay on the floor. . . .

Once they arrived at the U.S. base (this was [forward operating base] Volturno near Fallujah) they were kept in a holding area with around forty other prisoners in a large room with several open windows. It was bitterly cold. . . .

Bags were alternately placed on their heads and taken off again. Deafening music was played on loudspeakers directly into their ears and they were told to dance around the room. Sometimes when they were doing this, soldiers would shine very bright [flashlights] directly into their eyes and hit them with the [flashlights]. They were told to lie on the floor and wiggle their backsides in the air to the music. They were told to do repeated press ups and to repeatedly stand up from a crouching position and then return to the crouching position.

Soldiers would move between them, whispering things in their ear. . . . Salem says they whispered that they wanted to have sex with him and were saying "come on, just for two minutes." They also said he should bring his wife so they could have sex with her. . . .

Soldiers would whisper in their ears "One, two, three ..." and then shout something loudly right beside their ear. All of this went on all night.... Ahmad said he collapsed by morning. Sattar said he collapsed after Ahmad and began vomiting....

When they were taken individually for interrogation, they were interrogated by two American soldiers and an Arab interpreter. All three shouted abuse at them. They were accused of shooting down the helicopter. Salem, Ahmad, and Sattar all reported that for their first interrogation they were told to kneel on the floor with their feet raised off the floor and with their hands raised in the air.

If they let their feet or hands drop they were slapped and shouted at. Ahmad said he was forced to insert a finger into his anus and lick it. He was also forced to lick and chew a shoe. For some of the interrogation tissue paper was placed in his mouth and he had difficulty breathing and speaking. Sattar too said he was forced to insert a finger into his anus and lick it. He was then told to insert this finger in his nose during questioning, still kneeling with his feet off the ground and his other arm in the air. The Arab interpreter told him he looked like an elephant....

Ahmad and Sattar both said that they were given

badges with the letter "C" on it. They did not know what the badges meant but whenever they were being taken from one place to another in the base, if any soldier saw their badge they would stop to slap them or hurl abuse.[9]

Different soldiers, different unit, different base; and yet it is obvious that much of what might be called the "thematic content" of the abuse is very similar: the hooding, the loud noises, the "stress positions," the sexual humiliations, the threatened assaults, and the forced violations—all seem to emerge from the same script, a script so widely known that apparently even random soldiers the Reuters staffers encountered in moving about the Volturno base knew their parts and were able to play them. All of this, including the commonly recognized "badge," suggests a clear program that had been purposely devised and methodically distributed with the intention, in the words of General Sanchez's October 12 memorandum, of helping American troops "manipulate an internee's emotions and weaknesses."

3.

I think what happened is that you took a sophisticated concept at Gitmo, where the Geneva Convention did not apply ... and you put it in the hands of people [in Iraq] who should have been driving trucks, or doing something else instead of guarding prisoners. It was a disaster waiting to happen.

> —Senator Lindsey Graham (R-S.C.),
> Armed Services Committee

What "sophisticated concept" does Senator Graham have in mind? How can what seems to be random and bizarre brutality possibly be described as "sophisticated?"

Though we are limited here to what is publicly known, as Senator Graham with his security clearances is not, it is still possible to chart, in the history of "extreme interrogation" since the late '50s, a general move toward more "scientific" and "touchless" techniques, the lineaments of which are all too evident in the morbid accounts now coming out of Iraq. The most famous compilation of these techniques can be found in the CIA's manual *KUBARK Counterintelligence Interrogation,* produced in 1963, and in particular its chapter "The Coercive Counterintelligence Interrogation of Resistant Sources," which includes the observation that:

All coercive techniques are designed to induce regression. . . . The result of external pressures of sufficient intensity is the loss of those defenses most recently acquired by civilized man. . . . "Relatively small degrees

29

of homeostatic derangement, fatigue, pain, sleep, loss,
or anxiety may impair these functions."[10]

The intent of such "homeostatic derangement," according
to the CIA manual, is to induce "the debility-dependence-
dread state," causing the prisoner to experience the "emotional and motivational reactions of intense fear and
anxiety...."

> The circumstances of detention are arranged to
> *enhance within the subject his feelings of being cut off from*
> *the known and the reassuring, and of being plunged into*
> *the strange ..."* Control of the source's environment
> permits the interrogator to determine his diet, sleep
> pattern and other fundamentals. Manipulating these
> into irregularities, so that the subject becomes disori-
> entated, is very likely to create feelings of fear and
> helplessness. [emphasis added]
>
> Thus the hooding, the sleep deprivation, the irreg-
> ular and insufficient meals, and the exposure to
> intense heat and cold. As a later version of the man-
> ual puts it, the "questioner" is able to manipulate the
> subject's environment, to create unpleasant or intol-
> erable situations, to disrupt patterns of time, space,
> and sensory perception.... Once this disruption is

achieved, the subject's resistance is seriously impaired. He experiences a kind of psychological shock, which may only last briefly, but during which he is far ... likelier to comply.... Frequently the subject will experience a feeling of guilt. *If the "questioner" can intensify these guilt feelings, it will increase the subject's anxiety and his urge to cooperate as a means of escape.*[11] [emphasis added]

Viewed in this light, the garish scenes of humiliation pouring out in the photographs and depositions from Abu Ghraib—the men paraded naked down the cellblock with hoods on their heads, the forced masturbation, the forced homosexual activity, and all the rest—begin to be comprehensible; they are in fact staged operas of fabricated shame, intended to "intensify" the prisoner's "guilt feelings, increase his anxiety and his urge to cooperate." While many of the elements of abuse seen in the reports from Iraq, particularly the sensory deprivation and "stress positions," resemble methods used by modern intelligence services, including the Israelis and the British in Northern Ireland, some of the techniques seem clearly designed to exploit the particular sensitivities of Arab culture to public embarrassment, particularly in sexual matters.

The American military, of course, is well aware of these

cultural sensitivities; last fall, for example, the Marine Corps offered to its troops, along with a weeklong course on Iraq's customs and history, a pamphlet which included these admonitions:

> Do not shame or humiliate a man in public. Shaming a man will cause him and his family to be anti-Coalition.
>
> The most important qualifier for all shame is for a third party to witness the act. If you must do something likely to cause shame, remove the person from view of others.
>
> Shame is given by placing hoods over a detainee's head. Avoid this practice.
>
> Placing a detainee on the ground or putting a foot on him implies you are God. This is one of the worst things we can do.
>
> Arabs consider the following things unclean:
>
> Feet or soles of feet.
>
> Using the bathroom around others. Unlike Marines, who are used to open-air toilets, Arab men will not shower/use the bathroom together.
>
> Bodily fluids....[12]

These precepts, intended to help Marines get along with the Iraqis they were occupying by avoiding doing anything, however unwittingly, that might offend them, are turned precisely on their heads by interrogators at Abu Ghraib and other American bases. Detainees are kept hooded and bound; made to crawl and grovel on the floor, often under the feet of the American soldiers; forced to put shoes in their mouths. And in all of this, as the Red Cross report noted, the *public* nature of the humiliation is absolutely critical; thus the parading of naked bodies, the forced masturbation in front of female soldiers, the confrontation of one naked prisoner with one or more others, the forcing together of naked prisoners in "human pyramids." And all of this was made to take place in full view not only of foreigners, men and women, but also of that ultimate third party: the ubiquitous digital camera with its inescapable flash, there to let the detainee know that the humiliation would not stop when the act itself did but would be preserved into the future in a way that the detainee would not be able to control. Whatever those taking them intended to do with the photographs, for the prisoners the camera had the potential of exposing his humiliation to family and friends, and thus served as a "shame multiplier," putting enormous power in the hands of the interrogator. The prisoner must please his interrogator, else his shame would be unending.

If, as the manuals suggest, the road to effective interrogation lay in "intensifying guilt feelings," and with them "the subject's anxiety and his urge to cooperate as a means of escape," then the bizarre epics of abuse coming out of Abu Ghraib begin to come into focus, slowly resolving from what seems a senseless litany of sadism and brutality to a series of actions that, however abhorrent, conceal within them a certain recognizable logic. Apart from the Reuters report, we don't know much about what went on in the interrogation rooms themselves; up to now, the professionals working within those rooms have mostly refused to talk.[13] We do know, from the statements of several of the military policemen, that the interrogators gave them specific instructions: "Loosen this guy up for us. Make sure he has a bad night. Make sure he gets the treatment." When one of these soldiers, Sergeant Javal S. Davis, was asked why he didn't protest the abusive behavior, he answered that he "assumed that if they were doing anything out of the ordinary or outside the guidelines, someone would have said something. Also, the wing belongs to [Military Intelligence] and it appeared that MI personnel approved the abuse." He went on, speaking about one of the other accused policemen:

The MI staffs, to my understanding, have been giving Graner compliments on the way he has been handling

34

the MI holds [i.e., prisoners held by military intelligence]. Example being statements like "Good job, they're breaking down real fast;" "They answer every question;" "They're giving out good information, finally;" and "Keep up the good work"—stuff like that.[14]

As a lawyer for another of the accused, Staff Sergeant Ivan Fredericks, told reporters,

The story is not necessarily that there was a direct order. Everybody is far too subtle and smart for that.... Realistically, there is a description of an activity, a suggestion that it may be helpful and encouragement that this is exactly what we needed.

These statements were made by accused soldiers who have an obvious motive to shift the blame. Though few in military intelligence have spoken, and three have reportedly claimed the equivalent of Fifth Amendment protection,[15] one who has talked to journalists, Sergeant Samuel Provance, confirmed Sergeant Davis's assertion that the policemen were following orders:

> Military intelligence was in control. Setting the conditions for interrogations was strictly dictated by military intelligence. They weren't the ones carrying it out, but they were the ones telling the MPs to wake the detainees up every hour on the hour. . . .

Provance told the reporters that "the highest ranking officers at the prison were involved and that the Army appears to be trying to deflect attention away from the military intelligence's role."[16]

One needn't depend on the assertions of those accused to accept that what happened in Abu Ghraib and elsewhere in Iraq was not the random brutality of "a few bad apples" (which, not surprisingly, happens to be the classic defense governments use in torture cases). One needn't depend on the wealth of external evidence, including last fall's visit to Abu Ghraib by Major General Geoffrey Miller, then the commander of Guantanamo (and now commander of Abu Ghraib), in which, according to the Taguba report, he "reviewed current Iraqi Theater ability to rapidly exploit internees for actionable intelligence";[17] or Lieutenant General Sanchez's October 12 memorandum, issued after General Miller's visit, instructing intelligence officers to work more closely with military policemen to "manipulate an internee's emotions and weaknesses"; or statements from Thomas M. Pappas, the colonel in charge of intelligence, that he felt "enormous pressure," as the insurgency increased in intensity, to "extract more information from prisoners."[18] The internal evidence—the awful details of the abuse itself and the clear logical narrative they take on when set against what we know of the interrogation methods of the American military and intelligence agencies—is quite enough to show that what happened at Abu Ghraib, whatever it was, did not depend on the sadistic ingenuity of a few bad apples.

This is what we know. The real question now, as so often, is not what we know but what we are prepared to do.

4.

Should we remain in Algeria? If you answer "yes," then you must accept all the necessary consequences.
—Colonel Philippe Mathieu,
The Battle of Algiers (1965)

When, as a young intelligence officer, the late General Paul Aussaresses arrived in war-torn Algeria a half-century ago and encountered his first captured insurgent, he discovered that methods of interrogation were widely known and fairly simple:

> When I questioned them I started by asking what they knew and they clearly indicated that they were not about to talk. . . .
>
> Then without any hesitation, the policemen showed me the technique used for "extreme" interrogations: first, a beating, which in most cases was enough; then other means, such as electric shocks . . . ; and finally water. Torture by electric shock was made possible by generators used to power field radio transmitters, which were extremely common in Algeria. Electrodes were attached to the prisoner's ears or testicles, then electric charges of varying intensity were turned on. This was apparently a well-known procedure. . . .[19]

Aussaresses remarks that "almost all the French soldiers who served in Algeria knew more or less that torture was being used but didn't question the methods because they didn't have to face the problem directly." When as a responsible officer he gives a full report to his commander on his methods— which are yielding, as he notes, "very detailed explanations and other names, allowing me to make further arrests"— he encounters an interesting response:

> "Are you sure there aren't other ways of getting people to talk?" he asked me nervously. "I mean methods that are ..."
>
> "Faster?" I asked.
>
> "No, that's not what I mean."
>
> "I know what you mean, Colonel. You're thinking of cleaner ways. You feel that none of this fits in with our humanistic tradition."
>
> "Yes, that's what I mean," answered the Colonel.
>
> "Even if I did agree with you, sir, to carry out the mission you've given me, I must avoid thinking in moral terms and only do what is most useful."

Aussaresses's logic is that of a practical soldier: a traditional army can defeat a determined guerrilla foe only through superior intelligence; superior intelligence can be wrested from hardened insurgents in time to make it "actionable" only through the use of "extreme interrogation"—torture; therefore, to have a chance of prevailing in Algeria the French army must torture. He has nothing but contempt for superior officers, like his colonel, who quail at the notion of "getting their hands dirty"—to say nothing of the politicians who, at the least sign of controversy over the methods he is obliged to employ, would think nothing of abandoning him as "a rotten apple."

It has long since become clear that President Bush and his highest officials, as they confronted the world on September 11, 2001, and the days after, made a series of decisions about methods of warfare and interrogation that General Aussaresses, the practical soldier, would have well understood. The effect of those decisions—among them, the decision to imprison indefinitely those seized in Afghanistan and elsewhere in the war on terror, the decision to designate those prisoners as "unlawful combatants" and to withhold from them the protections of the Geneva Convention, and finally the decision to employ "high pressure methods" to extract "actionable intelligence" from them—was officially to transform the United States from a nation that did not torture to one that did. And the decisions were not, at least in their broad outlines, kept secret. They were known to officials of the other branches of the government, and to the public.

The direct consequences of those decisions, including details of the methods of interrogation applied in Guantanamo and at Bagram Air Base, began to emerge more than a year ago. It took the Abu Ghraib photographs, however, set against the violence and chaos of an increasingly unpopular war in Iraq, to bring Americans' torture of prisoners up for public discussion. And just as General Aussaresses would recognize some of the methods Americans are employing in their secret interrogation rooms—notably, the practice of "water-boarding," strapping prisoners down and submerging them until they are on the point of drowning, long a favorite not only of the French in Algeria but of the Argentines, Uruguayans, and others in Latin America[20]—the general would smile disdainfully at the contradictions and hypocrisies of America's current scandal over Abu Ghraib: the senior American officers in their ribbons prevaricating before the senators, the "disgust" expressed by high officials over what the Abu Ghraib photographs reveal, and the continuing insistence that what went on in Abu Ghraib was only, as President Bush told the nation, "disgraceful conduct by a few American troops, who dishonored our country and disregarded our values." General Aussaresses argued frankly for the necessity of torture but did not reckon on its political cost to what was, in the end, a political war. The general justified torture, as so many do, on the "ticking bomb" theory, as a means to protect lives immediately at risk; but in Algeria, as now in Iraq, torture, once sanctioned, is inevitably used much more broadly; and finally it becomes impossible to weigh what the practice gains militarily in "actionable intelligence" against what it loses politically, in an increasingly estranged population and an outraged world. Then as now, this was a political judgment, not a military one; and those who made it helped lose the generals' war.

A half-century later, the United States is engaged in another political war: not only the struggle against the insurgency in Iraq but the broader effort, if you credit the administration's words, to "transform the Middle East" so that "it will no longer produce ideologies of hatred that lead men to fly airplanes into buildings in New York and Washington." We can't know the value of the intelligence the torturers managed to extract, though top commanders admitted to *The New York Times* on May 27 that they learned "little about the insurgency" from the interrogations. What is clear is that the Abu Ghraib photographs and the terrible story they tell have done great damage to what was left of America's moral power in the world, and thus its power to inspire hope rather than hatred among Muslims. The photographs "do not represent America," or so the President asserts, and we nod our heads and agree. But what exactly does this mean? As so often, it took a comic, Rob Corddry on *The Daily Show with Jon Stewart,* to point out the grim contradiction in this:

There's no question what took place in that prison was horrible. But the Arab world has to realize that the U.S. shouldn't be judged on the actions of a . . . well, we shouldn't be judged on actions. It's our principles that matter, our inspiring, abstract notions. Remember: Just because torturing prisoners is something we did, doesn't mean it's something we *would* do.

Over the next weeks and months, Americans will decide how to confront what their fellow citizens did at Abu Ghraib, and what they go on doing at Bagram and Guantanamo and other secret prisons. By their actions they will decide whether they will begin to close the growing difference between what Americans say they are and what they actually do. Iraqis and others around the world will be watching to see whether all the torture will be stopped and whether those truly responsible for it, military and civilian, will be punished. This is, after all, as our President never tires of saying, a war of ideas. Now, as the photographs of Abu Ghraib make clear, it has also become a struggle over what, if anything, really does represent America.

—May 27, 2004
(This is the second of two articles)

1. "In Abu Ghraib prison alone, senior officials have testified that no less than three sets of interrogation policies were put in play at different times—those cited in Army field manuals, those used by interrogators who previously worked in Afghanistan and a third set created by Iraq's commanding general after policies used at Guantanamo Bay," from Craig Gordon, "High-Pressure Tactics: Critics Say Bush Policies—Post 9/11—Gave Interrogators Leeway to Push Beyond Normal Limits," *Newsday,* May 23, 2004.

2. See my "Torture and Truth," *The New York Review,* June 10, 2004, the first part of the present article, which takes up the Red Cross report in detail.

3. See Edward Epstein, "Red Cross Reports Lost, Generals Say: 'The System Is Broken,' Army Commander Tells Senate Panel about Abu Ghraib Warnings," *San Francisco Chronicle,* May 20, 2004.

4. See Douglas Jehl and Eric Schmitt, "Officer Says Army Tried to Curb Red Cross Visits to Prison in Iraq," *The New York Times,* May 19, 2004.

5. See R. Jeffrey Smith, "Memo Gave Intelligence Bigger Role: Increased Pressure Sought on Prisoners," *The Washington Post,* May 21, 2004.

6. See Douglas Jehl and Neil A. Lewis, "U.S. Disputed Protected Status of Iraq Inmates," *The New York Times,* May 23, 2004.

7. See Josh White and Scott Higham, "Sergeant Says Intelligence Directed Abuse," *The Washington Post,* May 20, 2004.

8. See "Translation of Sworn Statement Provided by _____, Detainee #_____, 1430/21 Jan 04," available along with thir-

teen other affidavits from Iraqis, at "Sworn Statements by Abu Ghraib Detainees," www.washingtonpost.com. The name was withheld by *The Washington Post* because the witness "was an alleged victim of sexual assault."

9. See Greg Mitchell, "Exclusive: Shocking Details on Abuse of Reuters Staffers in Iraq," *Editor and Publisher,* May 19, 2004, which includes excerpts from the Baghdad bureau chief's report.

10. See *KUBARK Counterintelligence Interrogation—July 1963,* archived at "Prisoner Abuse: Patterns from the Past," National Security Archive Electronic Briefing Book No. 122, p. 83; www.gwu.edu/~nsarchiv/NSAEBB/NSAEBB122. "KUBARK" is a CIA codename.

11. See *Human Resource Exploitation Training Manual—1983,* National Security Archive Electronic Briefing Book No. 122, "Non-coercive Techniques"; www.gwu.edu/~nsarchiv/NSAEBB/NSAEBB122.

12. See "Semper Sensitive: From a Handout That Accompanies a Weeklong Course on Iraq's Customs and History," Marine Division School, *Harper's,* June 2004, p. 26. For a discussion of shame and the American occupation of Iraq, see my "Torture and Truth."

13. Though we do know something of what has gone on at other American interrogation centers, for example, the American air base at Bagram, Afghanistan. See Don Van Natta Jr., "Questioning Terror Suspects in a Dark and Surreal World," *The New York Times,* March 9, 2003, and my "Torture and Truth."

14. See Scott Higham and Joe Stephens, "Punishment and Amusement," *The Washington Post*

15. Richard A. Serrano, "Three Witnesses in Abuse Case Aren't Talking: Higher-ups and a Contractor Out to Avoid Self-incrimination," *San Francisco Chronicle,* May 19, 2004.

16. See White and Higham, "Intelligence Officers Tied to Abuses in Iraq."

17. See General Antonio M. Taguba, "Article 15-6 Investigation of the 800th Military Police Brigade" (The Taguba Report), page 7.

18. See Douglas Jehl, "Officers Say U.S. Colonel at Abu Ghraib Prison Felt Intense Pressure to Get Inmates to Talk," *The New York Times,* May 18, 2004.

19. See Paul Aussaresses, *The Battle of the Casbah: Terrorism and Counter-Terrorism in Algeria, 1955–1957,* translated by Robert L. Miller (Enigma, 2002).

20. See James Risen, David Johnston, and Neil A. Lewis, "Harsh CIA Methods Cited in Top Qaeda Interrogations," *The New York Times,* May 13, 2004.

3.
Power and Vainglory

John Gray

Misguided from the start, the war in Iraq is spiraling out of control. Any legitimacy the occupying forces may ever have possessed has been destroyed, and there are signs that Iraqi insurgents are coming together to mount a movement of resistance that could render the country ungovernable. With even more damning images likely to find their way into the public realm in the near future, the United States is facing an historic defeat in Iraq—a blow to American power more damaging than it suffered in Vietnam, and far larger in its global implications.

The inescapable implication of currently available evidence is that the use of torture by U.S. forces was not an aberration, but a practice sanctioned at the highest levels. Undoubtedly there were serious breaches of discipline, and the blank failure to understand that they had done anything wrong displayed by some of the abusers does not speak well for the levels of training of sections of the U.S. military.

Abuse on the scale suggested by the Red Cross report cannot be accounted for by any mere lapse in discipline or the trailer-park mentality of some American recruits. It was inherent in the American approach to the war. American military intervention in Iraq was based on neoconservative fantasies about U.S. forces being greeted as liberators. In fact, as could before seen at the time, it has embroiled these forces in a brutal and hopeless war against the Iraqi people. From being regarded as passive recipients of American goodwill, they are now viewed as virtually subhuman. If, as seems clear, British forces are innocent of anything resembling the systemic abuse that appears to have been practiced by the Americans, one reason is that they do not share these attitudes.

The resistance mounted by the Iraqi insurgents can be compared to the anti-colonial liberation struggles of the 1950s, but the closest parallels with the intractable conflict now under way are found in Chechnya, which remains a zone of anarchy and terror despite the ruthless deployment of Russian firepower and the systematic use of torture for more than a decade. It was the prospect of an intractable guerrilla conflict that led many soldiers in the Pentagon to express deep reservations regarding the war. When the civilian leadership launched the invasion of Iraq, U.S. forces were plunged into a type of conflict for which they are supremely ill equipped.

In the wake of Vietnam and Somalia, American military doctrine has been based on "force protection" and "shock and awe." In practice, these strategies mean killing anyone who appears to pose any threat to U.S. forces and overcoming the enemy through the use of overwhelming firepower. Effective in the early stages of the war when the enemy was Saddam and his regime, they are deeply counterproductive when, as in Iraq today, the enemy comprises much of the population. As Douglas Hurd has observed, filling the hospitals and mortuaries is not the best way to win hearts and minds. The effect has been to make the conflict more savage. It is in circumstances such as these that torture becomes routine. In Iraq over the past year, as in Chechnya, and before that in Algeria where the French fought a similar dirty war, anyone could end up a victim of torture.

In subjecting randomly selected Iraqis to abuse, American forces are following a well-trodden path, but the type of torture that has been practiced has some distinctive features. Unlike the Russians or the French, who inflicted extremes of physical pain as well, U.S. forces in Iraq appear to be relying mainly on techniques that focus on the application of intense psychological pressure. In order to soften up detainees they have swept up from the streets, they have used disorientation, sensory deprivation, and sexual humiliation. These are all forms of abuse that would damage any human being, but leading naked Iraqi males around on dog

49

leashes and covering their heads with women's underwear look like techniques designed specifically in order to attack the prisoners' identity and values. The result is that an indelible image of American depravity has been imprinted on the entire Islamic world.

It remains unclear how these techniques came to be used in Abu Ghraib prison. What is evident is that from the start of the war on terror the Bush administration has flouted or circumvented international law on the treatment of detainees. It unilaterally declared members of terrorist organizations to be illegal combatants who are not entitled to the protection of the Geneva Convention. The detainees held at Guantanamo Bay fall into this category, and so apparently did the Taliban and al-Qaeda suspects who were captured in Afghanistan. Being beyond the reach of international law, they were liable to torture.

In Iraq, the Bush administration evaded international law by a different route. They outsourced security duties at Abu Ghraib and other American detention facilities to private contractors not covered by military law and not regulated by the Geneva Convention. In effect, the Bush administration deliberately created a lawless environment in which abuse could be practiced with impunity.

Some of the lawmakers who watched video stills of the sexual abuse of Iraqi women by U.S. personnel in a closed session on Capitol Hill in Washington last week have described the behavior they witnessed as un-American. Maybe so, but it was made possible by policies emanating from the highest levels of American leadership. The torture of Iraqis by U.S. personnel is an application of the Bush administration's strategy in the war on terror.

Tossing aside international law and the norms of civilized behavior in this way is self-defeating. Not so long ago, the clash of civilizations was just a crass and erroneous theory, but after the recent revelations it is becoming a self-fulfilling prophecy. In toppling Saddam, the Americans destroyed an essentially Western regime, not unlike the Stalinist Soviet Union in its militant secularism. In doing so, they empowered radical Islam as the single most important political force in the country.

The immediate beneficiary of the torture revelations is likely to be Iran—a fact that seems to have been grasped by Ahmed Chalabi (the Iraqi émigré that the neoconservatives believed would take the country to American-style democracy), who appears to be forging links with the Iranian regime. At a global level, the principal beneficiary is al-Qaeda, which is now a more serious threat than it has ever been.

The Bush administration's self-defeating approach to terrorism is symptomatic of a dangerous unrealism running right through its thinking. For Paul Wolfowitz, the Deputy Defense Secretary, and other neoconservatives, the solution to terrorism was to "modernize" the Middle East. For them, that meant overthrowing many, if not most, of the area's regimes and replacing them with secular liberal democracies. They appear not to have noticed that the region's secular regimes were authoritarian states such as Syria and Iraq. In the Middle East today, as in Algeria in the past, democracy means Islamist rule.

In part, the attack on Iraq was simply another exercise in the type of neo-Wilsonian fantasy that is a recurring feature of U.S. foreign policy, but it was also an exercise in realpolitik—and a resource war. A key part of the rationale for the invasion was to enable the U.S. to withdraw from Saudi Arabia, which had come to be seen as complicit with terror and inherently unstable.

If it was to pull out from Saudi Arabia, the U.S. needed another source of oil. Only Iraq has it in sufficient quantities—hence the drive for regime change. In this Dr. Strangelove-like vision, once Saddam had been removed and Iraq remodeled as a Western-style democracy, the oil would start flowing. The war would be self-financing, and the world economy would move smoothly into the sunlit uplands.

Things have not turned out quite like that. Oil prices have risen, not fallen, and they could easily rise further.

Partly this is a result of the increasingly desperate security situation in Iraq. The Americans did more than overthrow Saddam's despotic regime; they also destroyed the Iraqi state, with the result that the country is now in a condition of semi-anarchy.

Given the ill-judged attack by U.S. forces on the Shia holy city of Najaf and the likelihood that the beheading of Nicholas Berg by Islamist militants will be followed by more such atrocities, the level of violence in the country will almost certainly escalate. In that case, Iraq will be the scene of a mass exodus. International organizations and Western oil companies will leave and any prospect of rebuilding the country will be lost. Where will that leave Iraq—and its oil?

The exodus will not be confined to Iraq. Western companies are already leaving Saudi Arabia, the producer of last resort in the global oil market. Emboldened by the worsening situation in Iraq, forces linked to al-Qaeda have intensified their attacks on Saudi targets. Economists may say that the world need not fear another oil shock, but they have forgotten the geo-political realities. Saudi oil is still hugely important, and any sign of increased instability in the country is immediately reflected in the oil price. The impact of a major upheaval in the kingdom would be incalculable.

The U.S. cannot afford an ongoing war in Iraq, but the price of a quick exit will be high. Even so, it looks clear that

that is exactly what is about to happen. After the torture revelations, "staying the course" is no longer feasible. This is not because the American public has reacted with massive revulsion to evidence of the systematic abuse of Iraqis—as has been the case in Britain and other European countries. Rather, Iraq and its people are now viewed with a mix of bafflement and hatred, and a mood of despair about the war has set in. Most Americans want out—and soon. Locked in internal dispute, the Democrats have not so far been able to grasp the nettle. The pressure on President Bush to announce that America has completed its mission with the handover of sovereignty may well prove overwhelming.

If he decides to cut and run, Bush may yet survive the debacle in Iraq. No such prospect beckons for Tony Blair. It was his brand of messianic liberalism that dragged Britain into the war. For the Prime Minister, going to war in Iraq offered an intoxicating feeling of rectitude combined with the reassuring sense of being on the side of the big battalions. But American invincibility was a neoconservative myth, and the notion that Blair can survive the hideous fiasco that is unfolding in Iraq is as delusional as the thinking that led to the war in the first place. It cannot be long before he is irresistibly prompted to seek new avenues for his messianic ambitions.

In the U.S., American withdrawal will be represented as

a reward for a job well done. The rest of the world will recognize it as a humiliating defeat, and it is here that the analogy of Vietnam is inadequate. The Iraq war has been lost far more quickly than that in Southeast Asia, and the impact on the world is potentially much greater. Whereas Vietnam had little economic significance, Iraq is pivotal in the world economy. No dominoes fell with the fall of Saigon, but some pretty weighty ones could be shaken as the American tanks rumble out of Baghdad.

The full implications of such a blow to American power cannot be foreseen. One consequence is clear enough, however. The world has seen the last of liberal imperialism. It died on the killing fields of Iraq. It is no consolation to the people of that country, but at least their sufferings have demonstrated the cruel folly of waging war in order to fight a liberal crusade.

4.

An Old Refrain That Stabs at the Heart

Meron Benvenisti

The sights of Rafah are too difficult to bear—trails of refugees alongside carts laden with bedding and the meager contents of their homes; children dragging suitcases larger than themselves; women draped in black kneeling in mourning on piles of rubble. And in the memories of some of us, whose number is dwindling, arise similar scenes that have been a part of our lives, as a sort of refrain that stabs at the heart and gnaws at the conscience, time after time, for over half a century—the procession of refugees from Lod to Ramallah in the heat of July 1948; the convoys of banished residents of Yalu and Beit Nuba, Emmaus and Qalqilyah in June 1967; the refugees of Jericho climbing on the ruins of the Allen by Bridge after the Six-Day War.

And perhaps the most shocking of all, the grandfathers and fathers of the Rafah refugees, abandoning the houses in Yibna in which they were born, in fear of the approaching Israeli army on June 5, 1948. "At dawn," reported the Associated Press correspondent, "it was possible to see the civilians fleeing from the town [Yibna] in the direction of the coast, without the intervention of the Israeli attackers."

Some fifty-six years have passed, and they are again flee-ing in fear of the Israeli attackers.

And the attackers adopt the same tactics, spread rumors and fire warning shots; and when the residents flee out of fear, they claim that they are not responsible for the flight, but then destroy the homes, for "after all, they are empty and deserted."

Laundered language and sterile military terms camou-flage a primitive desire for vengeance and uninhibited mili-tancy. Slogans such as "combat heritage," "righteousness of our path," and "the most moral army in the world" immu-nize the soldiers and their commanders from having to con-tend with the humanitarian tragedy they are creating.

The political echelon, which is supposed to guide the army according to ethical criteria, reveals even crueler and more extreme tendencies that the commanders of the army. All they are interested in is the "image" of Israel and the condemnation of the "hostile media."

S. Yizhar has already said these harsh sentences about all of us: "To be deceived open-eyed, and to on the spot join the big, common throng of liars—composed of ignorance, expedient apathy, and simple unashamed selfishness—and to exchange one big truth for the clever shrug of the shoul-der of a veteran criminal." He said this in May 1949, in ref-erence to the incident at Khirbet Khiza'a, some of whose former residents live in one of the Rafah refugee camps.

The community of those seeking vengeance, and who crave "the appropriate response" will no doubt respond with anger and abuse: How can you show empathy for a bunch of base murderers, desert savages who are led by corrupt gang chieftains? But there is a sneaking suspicion that this too is "combat heritage"—exploitation of the murderousness of the Palestinians to "punish" them, uproot them from their homes, "bare" their fields, and then "redeem" the abandoned land for the needs of Israelis. Generation after generation, we cause them to abandon their homes, settling in them, and afterward, when the opportunity arises, take over their sanctuaries as well, and drive them away from there.

Generation after generation, we feed the refugee consciousness, reconstruct the pain of displacement, and expose another generation to the powerless rage of the displaced person. Afterward we face, frightened and threatened, the "return"—the life's hope of every refugee and a stain on the settler's conscience.

Something basic has gone awry here. If commanders, the sons of the fighters of 1948, send the grandchildren of the fighters for independence to "widen the route"—which means the expulsion of the grandchildren of the refugees of 1948—on the pretext of existential threat, then there was something defective in the vision of the founding fathers.

If after a half-century their enterprise still faces existential threat, this can only mean that they condemned it to eternal enmity, and there is no community that can for years on end survive a violent war for its existence.

And if this is merely a pretext—and Operation Rainbow in Rafah was an instinctive reaction that evolved into second nature—we must reflect deeply and sadly on our own responsibility for the enterprise that at its start embodied so many exalted ideals.

Is there some "original sin" that lies at the foundation of the Zionist enterprise? Those who initiated the Rafah operation, and those who are executing it, should know that one of the outcomes of their actions will inevitably be the raising of questions about this heresy.

5.
Abu Ghraib: The Surround

David Matlin

There is a cold stench coming off of the pictures from Abu Ghraib prison. President Bush claims that these images do not represent America and nearly all of the comments by either our politicians or media spokespersons fail to grasp the most dangerous connections between these pictures and our domestic policies of massive prison construction over the last twenty-year period. I find myself in near despair writing this editorial because these images are the images of ourselves we have, at now unimaginable costs, either ignored or tragically embraced inside our own society for decades.

The pictures of our young men and women "loosening up" prisoners are part of the secret ransoms of our daily lives we have chosen to place at the most conveniently distant moral boundaries hidden from either our questions or the painful glare of our indifferences. There is also another picture I am looking at of Paul Wolfowitz "touring" the newly refurbished jail cells of Abu Ghraib, in the spring of 2003, encoded with the certainties of his own culture which imprisons over 2 million prisoners, fully one-quarter of the world's prison population. I am also looking at pictures

(published by *The New York Times*) of small steel cages or SPAs (secure program areas) California juvenile offenders are thrown into; these are images of barbarity and inhumanity. Or am I thinking of prisoners in Maryland chained at wrist and ankle and thrown into cells with a hole in the middle of the floor for urine and feces, who experience such isolation that they can only in last resort try to stab the hands that torment them for human contact; or am I remembering the horror tales of forced gladiatorial combat in the prisons of California, my home state, where in the face of massive budget cuts the only "entity" to received increases is prisons which presently house over 162,000 persons. Kings County in California, for instance, is the largest county in the United States where presently more than 10 percent of the population are prisoners.

Lassen County has a population of 35,000; 10,500 are prisoners. The math, though easy at a simple calculable level, should produce nothing but unease but we as a People have chosen to imprison and maintain a catastrophic subworld of punishment and security which have, in turn, become deadening manmade hells which haunt and drain us of our ethics and our deepest Democratic conduct, as well as the humanitarian purposes of our treasury. "Jail Cam," a station in Phoenix, Arizona, was recently designed for "educational and deterrent purposes" as defined by the "nation's toughest sheriff," Joe Arpaio. Its cameras featured female inmates using a toilet, each view Internet accessible, as introduced by this new breed of admired XXXLawman, whose fame includes the reintroduction of desert chaingangs in stripped uniforms forcing convicts to wear pink underwear in his version of cost-track stud territory. I find absolutely no joy in presenting the following numbers, nor do I find any reassurance in President Bush's claims about his version of the identity of either myself or ourselves as Americans.

In 2000, 791,600 black men were in jail or prison in America while 603,032 were enrolled in universities or colleges. In 1980, by contrast, 143,000 black men were in our jails while 463,000 were in colleges or universities. During the prison-building boom of the last twenty years the number of Americans of all races and gender in our jails or prisons has quadrupled from 582,000 in 1980 to over 2.1 million in 2000, and the numbers have not gone down. The juvenile justice system in the State of California abounds in strange numbers that pose equally strange questions over our supposed Democratic longings and crafts. Youth of color number 83 percent of those wards going to adult courts. The recidivism rates for children who enter these gates is both a disheartening and bewildering 90 percent. Out of the 9 percent who did not reenter the system, 2 percent were known to be dead in reviews conducted in 2004. The cost per year to house each juvenile offender is $80,000 and youth detention facilities in California are fertility symbols for violence, hatred, increased criminal behavior, and either a reduced lifespan or no life, since condemnation to these spaces is a multidimensional death sentence few of us ever see.

Though I haven't really begun to find the range of this story, unspeakable as it is, the images from Abu Ghraib nonetheless are the unsayable whispers of our own invention heaving with wanton violation. Perhaps we should be more fearful that this is a portrait of our supposed Democratic Selves in a collective vocation of "innocence" and "optimism" shattering our Constitution and the vision of public trust this all too human document once allowed us to embrace. Has our normalization of prison and its economics made such trust impossible, and will the historically allowable invasions of cruelty and the yearning for more and more cruelty as witnessed by our embrace of prisons place the recovery of a public trust into a distance we may, even now, never be able to recompose? The form and signature of these immeasurable losses invades the images from Abu Ghraib and now, more than at any other time in our history, those images humiliate and set us adrift. Make no mistake; these are ugly, dangerous facts about who we may be and who we think we are. In Texas, there are the Choirs who stand outside of prisons while convicts are being given lethal injections and serenade the about-to-die with "Happy Trails Again." I hope the unquestioned ease of such barbarous cruelty does not mean that we have become a People no longer safe from ourselves who will look for any hidden means possible to trivialize our most lawfully malevolent impulses, as those impulses harm and poison others.

6.
Feminism's Assumptions Upended

Barbara Ehrenreich

Even those people we might have thought were impervious to shame, like the secretary of Defense, admit that the photos of abuse in Iraq's Abu Ghraib prison turned their stomachs.

The photos did something else to me, as a feminist: They broke my heart. I had no illusions about the U.S. mission in Iraq—whatever exactly it is—but it turns out that I did have some illusions about women.

Of the seven U.S. soldiers now charged with sickening forms of abuse in Abu Ghraib, three are women: Spc. Megan Ambuhl, Pfc. Lynndie England, and Spc. Sabrina Harman.

It was Harman we saw smiling an impish little smile and giving the thumbs-up sign from behind a pile of hooded, naked Iraqi men as if to say, "Hi Mom, here I am in Abu Ghraib!" It was England we saw with a naked Iraqi man on a leash. If you were doing PR for al-Qaeda, you couldn't have staged a better picture to galvanize misogynist Islamic fundamentalists around the world.

Here, in these photos from Abu Ghraib, you have everything that the Islamic fundamentalists believe characterizes Western culture, all nicely arranged in one hideous image of imperial arrogance, sexual depravity, and gender equality.

Maybe I shouldn't have been so shocked. We know that good people can do terrible things under the right circumstances. This is what psychologist Stanley Milgram found in his famous experiments in the 1960s. In all likelihood Ambuhl, England, and Harman are not congenitally evil people. They are working-class women who wanted an education and knew that the military could be a steppingstone in that direction. Once they had joined, they wanted to fit in.

And I also shouldn't be surprised because I never believed that women were innately gentler and less aggressive than men. Like most feminists, I have supported full opportunity for women within the military 1) because I knew women could fight, and 2) because the military is one of the few options around for low-income young people.

Although I opposed the 1991 Persian Gulf War, I was proud of our servicewomen and delighted that their presence irked their Saudi hosts. Secretly, I hoped that the presence of women would over time change the military, making it more respectful of other people and cultures, more capable of genuine peacekeeping. That's what I thought, but I don't think that anymore.

A certain kind of feminism, or perhaps I should say a

certain kind of feminist naiveté, died in Abu Ghraib. It was a feminism that saw men as the perpetual perpetrators, women as the perpetual victims, and male sexual violence against women as the root of all injustice. Rape has repeatedly been an instrument of war and, to some feminists, it was beginning to look as if war was an extension of rape. There seemed to be at least some evidence that male sexual sadism was connected to our species' tragic propensity for violence. That was before we had seen female sexual sadism in action.

But it's not just the theory of this naive feminism that was wrong. So was its strategy and vision for change. That strategy and vision rested on the assumption, implicit or stated outright, that women were morally superior to men. We had a lot of debates over whether it was biology or conditioning that gave women the moral edge or simply the experience of being a woman in a sexist culture. But the assumption of superiority, or at least a lesser inclination toward cruelty and violence, was more or less beyond debate. After all, women do most of the caring work in our culture, and in polls are consistently less inclined toward war than men.

I'm not the only one wrestling with that assumption today. Mary Jo Melone, a columnist for the *St. Petersburg Times,* wrote on May 7:

> I can't get that picture of England [pointing at a hooded Iraqi man's genitals] out of my head because this is not how women are expected to behave. Feminism taught me thirty years ago that not only had women gotten a raw deal from men, we were morally superior to them.

If that assumption had been accurate, then all we would have had to do to make the world a better place—kinder, less violent, more just—would have been to assimilate into what had been, for so many centuries, the world of men. We would fight so that women could become the generals, CEOs, senators, professors, and opinion-makers and that was really the only fight we had to undertake. Because once they gained power and authority, once they had achieved a critical mass within the institutions of society, women would naturally work for change. That's what we thought, even if we thought it unconsciously and it's just not true. Women can do the unthinkable.

You can't even argue, in the case of Abu Ghraib, that the problem was that there just weren't enough women in the military hierarchy to stop the abuses. The prison was directed by a woman, Brig. Gen. Janis Karpinski. The top U.S. intelligence officer in Iraq, who also was responsible for reviewing the status of detainees before their release, was Major Gen. Barbara Fast. And the U.S. official ultimately responsible for managing the occupation of Iraq since October was Condoleezza Rice. Like Donald H. Rumsfeld, she ignored repeated reports of abuse and torture until the undeniable photographic evidence emerged.

What we have learned from Abu Ghraib, once and for all, is that a uterus is not a substitute for a conscience. This doesn't mean gender equality isn't worth fighting for for its own sake. It is. If we believe in democracy, then we believe in a woman's right to do and achieve whatever men can do and achieve, even the bad things. It's just that gender equality cannot, all alone, bring about a just and peaceful world.

In fact, we have to realize, in all humility, that the kind of feminism based on an assumption of female moral superiority is not only naive; it also is a lazy and self-indulgent form of feminism. Self-indulgent because it assumes that a victory for a woman, a promotion, a college degree, the right to serve alongside men in the military, is by its very nature a victory for all of humanity. And lazy because it assumes that we have only one struggle—the struggle for gender equality—when in fact we have many more.

The struggles for peace and social justice and against imperialist and racist arrogance, cannot, I am truly sorry to say, be folded into the struggle for gender equality.

What we need is a tough new kind of feminism with no illusions. Women do not change institutions simply by assimilating into them, only by consciously deciding to fight for change. We need a feminism that teaches a woman to say no, not just to the date rapist or overly insistent boyfriend, but, when necessary, to the military or corporate hierarchy within which she finds herself.

In short, we need a kind of feminism that aims not just to assimilate into the institutions that men have created over the centuries, but to infiltrate and subvert them.

To cite an old, and far from naive, feminist saying: "If you think equality is the goal, your standards are too low." It is not enough to be equal to men, when the men are acting like beasts. It is not enough to assimilate. We need to create a world worth assimilating into.

7.
Abu Ghraib and a New Generation of Soldiers

Brooke Warner

An opportunity to visit Pakistan in 1995 was my first encounter with a developing country, a devoutly Muslim country where the people woke up before sunrise to pray and
where I, as a young Western woman, was told in quick
hushed reprimands that eye contact with men served to confirm the rumors that American women are too promiscu-
ous and liberal. I was wholly unprepared for so much of my
trip, a vacation of sorts. I went with a Pakistani-American
I had known all through high school and college. I was close
to her family and understood some of their traditions and
customs. But growing up female in the United States does
not prepare even the most well-read or culturally enlight-
ened among us for the vast differences—the cultural differences of a Muslim country, the economic disparity
between the U.S. and the developing world, or the social
inequality between men and women—that I would witness
firsthand. I grew up in the 1980s, having been born into the
America of the late 1970s when feminism was being alternately radicalized and sidelined, paving the way for a backlash that many women of my generation would contend

71

with as we came of age in a post-feminist United States.[1]
The Feminist Movement of the '60s and '70s created an
environment where young women like me expected to perform as well as men, achieve as much in the world, and be
respected for our minds and our choices.

My four-week stint in Pakistan was challenging and eye-
opening. To be a young white female in a country that has a
certain disdain for Western ideals is both intimidating and
educational. It was the first time in my life that I was judged
for the choices of my country—choices of which I was bliss-
fully unaware that had long ago planted the seeds of contempt
and resentment in row crops spanning an entire continent. I
was a foreigner in a country whose deep-seated cultural
wounds I didn't fully understand. But I was lucky. I was given
an initiation, a training course upon arrival that encouraged
understanding over fear and recognition over defensiveness.

This experience gave me pause when I read about young
female enlistees arriving in Iraq with inefficient resources
and lack of cultural awareness and historical perspective.
Young women shipping out to Iraq and Afghanistan
encounter the shock of poverty (visibly worse than what
one might witness among America's poorest), the public
inequality of women, disfigured children begging in the
streets, as well as anti-American sentiment and preconceived
notions about American women. Women soldiers are aware

of their vulnerability, even if that vulnerability is suppressed in order to prove the point that they indeed belong among the ranks of their fellow officers.[2] But women and men have far different military experiences, particularly in wartime. Women have historically been the victims of atrocities in wars since the earliest known battles. Kidnap and rape are routine costs of war. But so associated are these crimes with men that the revelations of the prison abuse at Abu Ghraib have caused a society-wide double take. This because the involvement of three young enlisted females found women on the wrong side of the violence.

According to the Bureau of Justice, the number of crimes committed by women has increased 140 percent since 1970. The young women who blithely posed for quick snapshots of themselves doing what most of us would imagine unthinkable are guilty perpetrators of crime and wartime atrocities, but also victims of the military environment, the circumstances of war, and modern American values. Private Lynndie England, age twenty-one, has received the most media coverage. Her own lawyer calls her "the poster child of Abu Ghraib." The lowest-ranking among the accused, England's callousness as she holds a slack leash attached to a man who lies naked on the floor is an indelible symbol of the prison abuse scandal. She is also the girlfriend of Specialist Charles Graner, age thirty-five, pregnant with his child and awaiting what will likely be a minimum fifteen-year sentence and a court-martial. Specialist Sabrina Harman is pictured—bright smile, latex glove sporting a thumbs-up—hovering over the exposed corpse of a man in a body bag. In another photo she is the Pollyanna face whose expression contradicts the fact that she is perched upon a pile of hooded naked men. Specialist Megan Ambuhl, age twenty-nine, also posed for a photo of detainees being held by leashes. Both Harman and Ambuhl face courts-martial. In an interview with the *Washington Post* in May 2004, England said that Graner and Frederick (another of the accused) motioned for her "to get beside him [a prisoner] and pose pointing at him masturbating for a picture.... I really didn't want to get close to him masturbating, but posed for the picture anyway."

Rush Limbaugh disturbingly called the behavior at Abu Ghraib nothing more than "a good time ... sort of like hazing, a fraternity prank. Sort of like that kind of fun." Fraternity-style good-time kicks? No. Adolescent-style acting out in a situation that was out of control? More likely. Perhaps the three women's transgressions are unique because of something the feminist movement worked toward but whose generation never completely embraced. But this generation gets it, lives it. Women are no longer the "delicate sex." Young women are tough, hard-edged, and aware of their power. The post-feminist world is an increasingly more violent world. Television, cinema, and videogames have had an effect, no matter what the media moguls claim to the contrary. A certain I-deserve-it attitude is commonplace among young American women who are encouraged to be strong, climb the corporate ladder, and strive for more. Brashness, confidence, and selfishness are norms in the fast-pace get-ahead culture where quickness of mind and assertion of one's opinions, if not admired, are certainly not met with wide-eyed shock. American military culture promotes these values as much as the university system, though it manifests itself as physical rather than intellectual prowess.

Salon writer Cathy Hong quoted neoconservative author Stephanie Guttman as saying, "Women can act just as badly as men. I think they have been aware of the Islamic attitude about women—which is not respectful. They may have subtly enjoyed being sadistic to the kind of men who enjoy humiliating other women." Sexual torture is about control and power, the most humiliating form of domination and dehumanization. The women accused of failing to protect prisoners and committing sadistic acts of abuse may have even seen their behavior as benign given the completely warped lens through which they were operating from day to day. If women prisoners were being raped and men shoved and kicked until they died from hemorrhages, then holding a leash attached to a groveling prisoner or posing on top of a pile of hooded bodies may have indeed seemed less cruel on the atrocity scale. However, the flashy smiles and complete disregard of the pain and torture make each and every picture appear surreal, as if the perpetrators superimposed photos from last summer's vacation onto a completely wretched scene. The fact that the officers seemingly didn't consider the impact such photos might create is perhaps the best evidence for their utter naïveté of the gravity of their actions.

Despite women's history of involvement in war, we know relatively little about the way women behave in wartime because they haven't been on the frontlines, confronted with the choice to pull the trigger, throw the grenade, the instant moment where you act for results—life or death. According to the Women's Research and Education Institute (WREI), "Since 1973, when the male draft ended and the All Volunteer Force began, the percentage of women among U.S. military personnel has increased dramatically, from 1.6 percent in 1973, to 8.5 percent in 1980, to 10.8 percent in 1989. Today, over 229,000 women serve on active duty in the military services." Despite these numbers, the list of grievances about women in the military is ongoing: women need time off for pregnancy; women take more bathroom breaks; women can't match up to men's physical standards; women are "feminizing" the military; women are more likely to get raped or sexually assaulted if they are taken prisoners. This list, compiled by Captain Barbara A. Wilson, USAF (Ret) in 1996, had the prescient response to the last point: "None of the military women taken prisoner in the Pacific in WWII were sexually assaulted. But the real answer is a question. Do you really think that male prisoners are NOT sexually tortured, raped, and sodomized?"

Lieut. Col. Dave Grossman's revealing book, *On Killing,* sets out to define a new area of study he terms "killology." The index lists only two entries for women: "killing of" and "as scapegoats." The primary entry reads: "*See also* rape." Sadly, the next edition will merit the inclusion of women as soldiers who engage in atrocities, having earned the dubious honor of further narrowing the gap between themselves and their male counterparts. Grossman cites emotional distance—cultural and moral—as being more determinative in the carrying out of killing and atrocities than actual physical distance between killer and target or victim. These are social and mental separations that allow the perpetrator "to deny that he is killing [or abusing] a human being." Cultural distancing is playing out with force in the war in Iraq because the America-Iraq conflict is a culture clash. More than looks, skin color, and dress, soldiers view mannerisms, cultural beliefs, and traditions as the true ground upon which they distinguish themselves as better and thus able to inflict pain and suffering. Though Grossman writes, "It is so much easier to kill [abuse] someone if they look distinctly different from you," emotional distancing happens irrespective of race or ethnicity. Stanley Milgram's 1960 obedience study at Yale and Phillip G. Zimbardo's 1971 Stanford Prison Experiment have been recalled in countless articles since the revelations of Abu Ghraib were made public. Both experiments showed the capacity of kind and caring people to act abominably under simulated circumstances, the former involving the presence of an authority figure ordering the infliction of harm, the latter studying the effect of arbitrarily dividing young men into guards and prisoners—the powerful and the powerless. The Stanford Experiment, in particular, involved exclusively white (and one Asian American) male students of similar age, background, and education levels.

In *On Killing,* an Israeli study is cited for its findings that a kidnapped victim is more likely to be killed if hooded. Photographs of Abu Ghraib's hooded victims are infamous legacies of interrogation policies gone awry. Former Army investigator Mike Ritz told *The New York Times,* "The use of hoods and sleep deprivation are 'common practice' techniques. You won't see that in print anywhere. It's one of those things that is understood but it's not discussed that much. It's something that has happened over time." The photograph on the cover of this book has become recognized internationally as the symbol of the Abu Ghraib scandal—a hooded man imprisoned for carjacking. Prisoner Satar Jabar's outstretched arms attached to shock wires, his precarious balance on a base so narrow that he has to stand with his feet touching, is so emblematic of the abuses that Iraqis contemptuously refer to it as "the Statue of Liberty."

Moral distancing is at the heart of Bush's "war on terror," which the Bush Administration has insisted is not a war on Islam, though with fairly low marks. Bush's own faith and religious rhetoric enforce the moral distancing that has served as the legitimizing factor for the war since its inception. Grossman writes, "The first component [of killing] is the determination and condemnation of the enemy's guilt, which, of course, must be punished or avenged. The other is an affirmation of the legality and legitimacy of one's own cause." The fact that the Iraq war is waged on such highfalutin moral grounds fits into Bush's I-felt-it-was-the-right-thing-to-do-in-my-heart rationale for war. Such rationale allows soldiers and ultimately those who commit abuses, or kill, to dismiss their guilt on the basis of morality and "doing the right thing." Yet to contrast Bush's "good" reasons with some that may leave most Americans feeling rather uncomfortable, Bush told King Abdullah of Jordan just before initiating action against Afghanistan, "Our nation is still somewhat sad, but we're angry. There's a certain level of blood lust, but we won't let it drive our reaction. We're steady, clear-eyed, and patient, but pretty soon we'll have to start displaying scalps."

Emotional distancing prevails even outside the pressure cooker of war. It is choosing to turn a blind eye to protect ourselves from the pain of seeing others suffer. It is dismissing the customs and traditions of another culture with the notion that the way we do it is better. It is the faithful asserting without qualms that their religion is the only true religion and that all non-believers are going to hell. And though empathy is the most resounding quality Americans have for countering emotional distancing, military training works hard to squash it. Reserve Brig. Gen. Janis Karpinksi, who was in charge of all sixteen U.S. prisons in Iraq, spoke out against Maj. Gen. Geoffrey Miller, Chief of Interrogations and Prisons in Iraq, saying, "He said they are like dogs, and if you allow them to believe at any point they are more than a dog then you've lost control of them."

Recently I had a conversation with Kurt Sveltely, who served four years in the Army and achieved the rank of Staff Sargeant during that time.[3] He recalled that supervisors taught them to dehumanize the enemy, to call them "it" to distance the soldiers from what they had to do. "Kill or be killed," he said matter-of-factly, and this from a man who never made it to combat. When I asked his take on the Abu

Ghraib scandal his response was thoughtful. "It does seem like they're having fun with it, but that kind of behavior is not encouraged in the military. The accused were all lower-level management and work forces. They were all enlisted. But you can't understand it until you're there. It's an ugly job to have to do, but until you're in that situation, following orders, defending your country, in fear of losing your life, you can never really know."

It's easy to speculate about what we might have done or how we might have acted in the same circumstances, but most of the critics and pundits have never served time in the military. Grossman, a soldier of twenty years' service, doesn't blame those who commit atrocities and kill. He argues that it is systemic: "It seems that when a society does not have natural processes (such as sex, death, and killing) before it, that society will respond by denying and warping that aspect of nature. As our technology insulates us from a specific aspect of reality, our societal response seems to be to slip deep into bizarre dreams about that which we flee. Dreams spun from the fantasy stuff of denial. Dreams that can become dangerous societal nightmares as we sink deeper into their tempting web of fantasy."

The Bush Administration has unsuccessfully maintained that the handful of abusers was limited to a few sick individuals (which, incidentally, now implicates twenty-seven rather than seven bad apples: these include mid-level officers and civilian contractors, at least one of whom has been indicted on charges in the death of a detainee in Afghanistan; several top military officers, including Lieut. Gen. Ricardo Sanchez, responsible but not culpable, who is being replaced this summer, 2004, although the military claims that this would have been a standard transfer regardless of the abuses; and finally Secretary of Defense Donald Rumsfeld himself, who has been fingered by Brig. Gen. Karpinski as the high-ranking voice that personally approved the introduction of harsher conditions of detention in Iraq). Lieut. Gen. Paul T. Mikolashek has been toeing the party line, blaming what is now twenty detainee deaths and seventy-four other cases of abuse—physical and sexual—on "the failure of individuals to follow known standards of discipline and Army values, and in some cases, the failure of a few leaders to enforce those standards of discipline." In a later quote he said, "These abuses should be viewed as what they are—unauthorized actions taken by a few individuals."

In June 2004, President Bush bristled in response to criticism about methods used to interrogate terrorism suspects held in the United States, "We're a nation of law. We adhere to laws. We have laws on the books. You might look at those laws, and that might provide comfort to you. And those were the instructions from me to the government." Most people probably do not feel comforted in light of Abu Ghraib. The public wants the soldiers to be held accountable for their actions, but they also want the Bush Administration to do its duty and see the process through. Anthony Lewis wrote in *The New York Review of Books* that "the situation calls for a criminal investigation by an independent prosecutor armed with subpoena power—and with the ethical commitment of such a person as Archibald Cox."

The hardest part to swallow in the aftermath of Abu Ghraib is how we, as a nation, continue to erode the confidence other countries—our once strong allies—have in us as a leader and bastion of moral certitude. In the 2004 presidential election, Bush and John Kerry are dragging Vietnam back into the forefront as each candidate seeks to discredit the other and extol his own virtues. Our candidates' lives and choices were deeply affected by Vietnam, an experience that should promote some small particle of wisdom in the way they handle young military recruits being sent to Iraq and Afghanistan. The current leaders who lived through Vietnam should be steering the new generation of soldiers away from the mistakes they witnessed, including atrocities, reactive decisions, and quick-fix solutions that were destined to fail. Instead they stare into the uncertainty of the future and indignantly make choices that can only serve to widen the divide with more hatred and misunderstanding and resentment.

The ramifications are great in terms of our relationships with other countries, but domestically the impact will also have a resounding effect. Excusing top military personnel from culpability, admitting that they only bore some responsibility, drives home the message of inequality. The great American divide exists stronger than ever in the divide between the classes, punishing those who don't have the resources to fight back. In Abu Ghraib it's the enlisted officers who will serve prison terms, bear the brunt of America's shame, and shoulder the blame that should be much more evenly accorded among senior officials. When I imagine Lynndie England, Sabrina Harman, and Megan Ambuhl, young women about my age, I imagine that they feel like they got sideswiped. The military did not live up to its end of the bargain. The accused are young and inexperienced. They arrived in Iraq, where, by Harman's account, there were no rules and little training. Outside the walls of Abu Ghraib was an entire nation that didn't want them there, a culture that has long resented America's involvement in the Middle East. The notion that the accused acted alone has been called preposterous and ludicrous. The American public is not that naïve. Donald Rumsfeld finally offered an apology in late July and took full responsibility for the prison abuses in Iraq. He then said, "It's going to get a good deal more terrible, I'm afraid." When Democrats suggested that he resign, he responded, "I would not resign simply because people try to make a political issue out of it."

The amount of attention that the prison abuse scandal has received worldwide is not a political issue. It is a harsh reality that America as a society and Americans as individuals will have to contend with for years to come. It has been nearly ten years since I was in the Middle East, and we are unquestionably worse off in the hearts and minds of the Muslim world than we were before 9/11. President Bush has argued time and time again in speeches all over the country that we are safer for having invaded Iraq. The fact that we haven't had an attack on U.S. soil since 9/11 means we are beating the terrorists. Time will tell. We have yet to see all the ramifications of the current Administration's policies. The United States will be reeling from this tragedy for decades after Bush leaves office, whether he serves another term or not. Abu Ghraib is one exposed boil on the sick body of America's current international policy. Only by making true attempts to understand and value each other's cultures can the West and the Middle East overcome the cultural distancing that is destroying relationships between both government and civilians. Both sides must promote understanding and respect, as well as cultural training courses for the military in order to mend the hatred whose pervasiveness is killing so many young people on both sides of the international divide.

In Iraq, the United States is promoting cultural distancing by cultivating our superiority and disvaluing a culture and a people whose deep roots and strong sense of pride does not see conforming to Western ideals as a possibility. In another thirty years, we will undoubtedly witness future presidential candidates revisit the heroism and blunders of the war in Iraq and the likely ongoing "war on terror." Key players in the outcome of these difficult times will resurface to lead our country into a future that will be forced to contend with random acts of terrorism and a culture of fear. If we embrace the values of the current administration we will see hardened men and women alike who will trivialize the importance of compassion and empathy and stand with unwavering determination against the backdrop of our inherited ignorance and the silenced wisdom of history.

1. The marginalization of feminism was the very product of its success. See: Susan Faludi. *Backlash: The Undeclared War Against American Women* (New York: Anchor Books, 1992).
2. Sociological research indicates that women in the armed forces play down their femininity. See Melissa S. Herbert. *Camouflage Isn't Only for Combat: Gender, Sexuality, and Women in the Military* (New York: New York University Press, 2000).
3. The sergeant's real name is not used.

8.

Breakdown in the Gray Room:
Recent Turns in the Image War

David Levi Strauss

For anyone who is fascinated by images and their social and political effects, these are heady times. From 9/11 on, visual images have had a tremendous influence on public perceptions and have often appeared to be the principal drivers of public opinion. Historians will say that this has been happening for awhile, but I would argue that the degree of this effect (in proportion to all other factors) has increased significantly since 9/11, and this makes it more important than ever to try to understand how it works. The only way I've found to do that is to try to slow the machinery down long enough to get a good look at its moving parts.

When I first saw the Abu Ghraib images, I didn't quite know what I was looking at. I didn't recognize them, because I'd never seen anything quite like them. One of the first people I discussed the images with was the painter Leon Golub. I asked him why the "detainees" were hooded. If the aim was humiliation and blackmail—which is what some claimed; that these photographs would be used to convince other prisoners to talk, under threat of receiving the same

treatment—it seemed like it would be better to be able to show their faces and identify them. And if they were strictly "trophy" images, for bragging rights back home, then why not show the terrified faces of your victims? Golub explained that these were torture images, and that the techniques pictured—hooding, forced nakedness, sexual humiliation, stress positions, dogs, etc.—were all common torture techniques, right out of the book. Hoods or blindfolds increase the sense of isolation and defenselessness. Essential to torture is the sense that your interrogators control everything: food, clothing, dignity, light, even life itself. Everything is designed to make it clear that you are at the mercy of those whose job it is not to have any mercy. Hooding victims dehumanizes them, making them anonymous and thing-like. They become just bodies. You can do anything you want to them.

One of the things that really drove home what Leon was telling me was a report that appeared in *The New York Times* soon after the Abu Ghraib images appeared on *60 Minutes II* and in the *New Yorker.*[1] The article reported on the immediate effects of these images on some of the 400,000 survivors of torture who have sought asylum in the U.S. More than 100,000 of them live in the New York area. When they saw the Abu Ghraib images, it was like flipping a switch. It awoke all the old traumas and also ignited a new fear for their own safety in America. These are people who came to the U.S. for refuge from torture, so to see the American government *engaged* in torture shook them to the core.

None of this was new to Leon Golub. He has been looking at, thinking about, and transforming this kind of material in his paintings for many years. Between 1979 and 1985, Golub represented the use of torture by repressive Central and South American regimes backed by the U.S. government, and by mercenaries helping them to interrogate subjects. Over the years, Leon has assembled a voluminous archive of images of interrogations and torture from around the world.

Right before the Abu Ghraib images were released, a series of images from Fallujah appeared, showing four "private security contractors" being ambushed, burned, mutilated, and hung from a bridge over the Euphrates as carrion.

The images from this gruesome unconscious reenactment of Goya's "Disasters of War" were circulating on the Internet within three hours of the acts, and their appearance the next day on the front pages of many U.S. newspapers and in the lead stories of most television news shows had a chilling effect. They recalled the images from Mogadishu in 1993, of a dead U.S. soldier's body being desecrated, which hastened the U.S. withdrawal from Somalia and prompted Osama bin Laden's reputed assertion that the American public cannot stomach this kind of imagery, making America a "weak horse." Surely the thugs on the streets of Fallujah had this in mind on March 31, 2004. They were enraged, but they were also clearly performing for the cameras, just as Chalabi's men had done a year earlier, when they toppled Saddam's statue in Firdos Square and symbolically mutilated his corpse and dragged it through the streets. The media consciousness of the Fallujah gang was apparent in their faces, and in the pre-printed signs they displayed, reading "Fallujah—the graveyard of Americans."

One of the reasons these ghastly images had such an effect in the U.S. was that they broke the embargo that the Bush administration, with the cooperation of the major American news media, had put on images that show the daily carnage in Iraq, an embargo extending even to images of the coffins of dead U.S. soldiers being returned to their families. No such censorship applies to the major media seen in Iraq, which regularly show the broken bodies of some of the 17,000 Iraqi men, women, and children killed in the war. The notion of a "clean" war, a war without carnage, is only saleable to a population that has been kept from seeing images of corpses.

But the effect of the Fallujah images was limited by Americans' ability to distance themselves from them. The *New York Post* ran the image of body parts festooning the bridge under the headline "SAVAGES," and Canada's *Globe and Mail* quoted an American woman as saying: "I'm sorry, but we don't do that here. We don't jump up and down on cars to celebrate the burning of human beings." When I read that, I immediately thought of the recent book *Without Sanctuary: Lynching Photographs in America,* examining in nauseating detail the widespread murder of African Americans in this country not so very long ago, the mutilation of their corpses, and the gleeful celebrations of the perpetrators being photographed beside their handiwork. As the executive editor of *The New York Times* said about the Fallujah images, "The story was in the desecration and in the jubilation."

Another effect of the Fallujah images was to reveal to the American public the prominence of hired, private military contractors in the Iraqi conflict; there are currently at least 20,000 of them in Iraq, and the number increases daily. The four men killed and mutilated by the mob in Fallujah were all former U.S. military Special Forces personnel turned private contractors, working under a Blackwater USA contract with the Pentagon to provide force protection and personal security for the top U.S. administrator in Iraq, Paul Bremer, among others. They were armed with assault rifles and automatic pistols. The Bush administration does not include the deaths of private military contractors in its death toll for the war, and uses these contractors to mask the real costs of the occupation.

Less than a month after the Fallujah images appeared, the release of a few amateur digital snapshots taken by soldiers changed everything in the image wars. These images showed American MPs "softening up" Iraqi detainees in the Sadean cells of Saddam Hussein's Abu Ghraib prison just outside Baghdad. The first batch, broadcast on CBS-TV's *60 Minutes II* on April 28, 2004, showed a dead, battered body—not burned, but packed in ice to escape detection—and the naked, hooded bodies of prisoners being tortured by grinning, gesticulating U.S. soldiers. The reality of these images was grasped immediately by all Iraqis under occupation, and then began to break on the American consciousness in successive waves of recognition and revulsion.

Unlike the Brits, who immediately questioned the veracity of the *Daily Mirror* images of prisoner abuse, we believed the Abu Ghraib images without question, because they only confirmed what we already knew but didn't want to accept: that behind all the pretty talk about wanting freedom for the good people of

Iraq lurked naked aggression, deep-seated cultural contempt, and the arrogant smirk of unilateralism, and the realization that we are now mired in a hellish conflict with no end in sight. The looks on the faces of those reservists, and their easy, hamming body postures, were intended to show that they, unlike the Iraqis, were not subject to the depredations of Abu Ghraib; that they were actually not there at all, but back home, mugging for the camera. The anonymous, hooded Iraqis (guilty or innocent, it hardly mattered) were demonstrably there, and were ridiculous for being there. Stripped and hooded, they'd become impotent and weak. Let's stack them up like cheerleaders. Let's make them jack-off in front of American women and make it look like they're giving each other head.

The most striking thing about the images from Abu Ghraib, and what marks them as unmistakably American, is that peculiar mixture of cold-blooded brutality and adolescent frivolity; of hazing or fooling around, and actual deadly torture—reality and fantasy conjoined. So you have Graner and England mugging and posing and grinning for the camera as if they're frolicking at Disneyland, and in the same picture you have the corpse of a prisoner who's been tortured to death. Most Americans didn't know what they were looking at when they first saw the images, because they'd never seen torture images before, and the incongruity of the actions of the U.S. soldiers was confusing. It was intended to be confusing. The MPs in the pictures wanted to show their friends and family back home that they were not affected by the ghastly acts they performed in Iraq; that they were not *above* these actions, but *below* them, just like their Commander-in-Chief, whose aw-shucks obliviousness to the grave consequences of his policy decisions is reassuring to some Americans. What we don't know can't hurt us. We're not responsible. They just hate us because we're free. Shit happens. And besides, it's God's will.

The Fallujah images arose from a public explosion of rage that was performed for and recorded by professional photojournalists, but the amateur images from Abu Ghraib seemed to have erupted from deep within the American public image unconscious. They seem not to have been taken by anyone, and at the same time, by us all. As Susan Sontag's

94

cover of *The New York Times Magazine* spelled it out, "The Photographs *Are* Us." And they put a face on the U.S. occupation of Iraq that will never be forgotten.

For an administration that had manipulated and controlled public images so skillfully during the first year of the war—from Saving Private Lynch to the Falling Saddam to the Top Gun speech to Saddam's capture—President Bush's closest advisors were blindsided by the effects of the Abu Ghraib images. Principal Bush political strategist Karl Rove suggested that the consequences of these images were so great that it would take decades for the U.S. to recover from them. Secretary of Defense Donald Rumsfeld's frustration was palpable as he testified before Congress: "We're functioning with peacetime constraints, with legal requirements, in a wartime situation in the Information Age, where people are running around with digital cameras and taking these unbelievable photographs and then passing them off, against the law, to the media, to our surprise." That is, we don't have a problem with how we are prosecuting this war, we have a problem with controlling images of the war. Paul Virilio's Big Optics (if you can *see* the entire battlefield, you've already won the battle) has gone public, and that creates a tremendous problem for the Pentagon. With the ubiquity of small, cheap digital cameras, this problem is probably now insoluble. What was once a tremendous military advantage has now become a political catastrophe. Conservative commentator David Brooks asked, "How are we going to wage war anymore, with everyone watching?" Could this be the apotheosis of Total Surveillance, the saving grace of the Pandaemonium?

As I said before, the Abu Ghraib images seemed to have welled up from the American public image unconscious. But why did these images have such an immediate and profound effect? Why were they so immediately legible?

Looking at the faces of these MPs from Maryland, I tried to find some comparable images, and a student of mine, Eric Gottesman, found a collection of images online that is certainly relevant. These images show revelers at "Blackface Parties" held at fraternity houses in Southern colleges and universities in the last few years. All of these images ignited public relations firestorms only after they were discovered on the Internet. These images come from Auburn University, the University of Virginia, University of Tennessee, Oklahoma State University, and the University of Mississippi, where an image of a man in blackface and straw hat kneeling on the floor picking cotton while a guard holds a gun to his head came out of the Alpha Tau Omega fraternity, which bills itself as "America's leadership development fraternity." The first fraternity founded after the Civil War, ATO's mission was "to heal the wounds created by

the devastating war and help reunite the North and South."

Another direct reference for the Abu Ghraib images is Do-It-Yourself Internet porn. A very high percentage of all traffic on the Internet is related to pornography. It's the sticky Web of Onan. And when members of Congress went into that dark, sweaty little room to view the whole cache of 1,800 images from Abu Ghraib, most of which *we* haven't yet seen, they said the torture images were all interspersed with pornographic images of the MPs themselves. So this is certainly a big part of what was going on there. Rush Limbaugh called it "Standard good old American pornography." Just a few good ol' boys and girls behaving badly.

Bush and Rumsfeld refuse to call what happened at Abu Ghraib torture, because torture is what other states do, not the U.S. If we're doing it, it must not be torture. Just as the tens of thousands of mercenaries now employed in Iraq must not be mercenaries, but "private military contractors," and setting up a satellite government to take the heat off the Occupation is "turning over sovereignty" to Iraqis. After Mogadishu, what we all saw happening in Rwanda was not "genocide," because we would have had to *do* something about genocide. This torturing (twisting) of language has become very effective of late, and has mostly managed to deflect language coming through to counter it. Image rhetorics have also been employed with great facility and effectiveness. So why and how did the Abu Ghraib images threaten this hegemony?

Like the earlier images of the Falling Saddam, these images draw on old image rhetorics, striking similar chords. But unlike those planned images, the Abu Ghraib images were *unconsciously* made, and this gave them a special power. As I said, these images seemed to have welled up out of our own unconscious, showing us what we knew, but didn't know that we knew.

The iconography of the hooded-figure-on-a-box image is especially, rampantly polysemous. It was legible to us because we immediately, unconsciously, recognized its symbolism. The pointed hat or hood carries the sense of derision and ridicule, as in the dunce cap, and also of judgment and punishment—the interrogators of the Spanish Inquisition wore pointed hats, as do KKK knights. The dunce cap was invented (by John Duns Scotus) as a device to aid cogitation, to "focus the mind," and the actions at Abu Ghraib were ostensibly designed to extract intelligence.

The pointed hood or hat is an ancient symbol and shamanic trope eliciting fear and respect that has inspired numerous artists, from Hugo Ball at the Cabaret Voltaire, to Alfred Jarry's Ubu Roi, to Joseph Beuys in his Coyote action, to Joel-Peter Witkin's early "Anonymous Atrocities" series.

On another level, to hood or shroud the head is a feminizing or emasculating gesture for Muslim men, and for Americans, the gesture of the hands held out in weakness and supplication in the Abu Ghraib figure echoes an earlier image of the victims of war: Nick Ut's image of the naked Vietnamese girl fleeing a napalm attack, with arms held out from her body like wings.

This one image of the hooded-figure-on-a-box has already become an icon, the image of the American Occupation of Iraq. There is certainly an element of initiation or hazing here (trying to get the pledges to break), but what are these Iraqis being initiated into? Our way—the perversion of the significance of events. Hazing is a devolution of initiation rituals, and both hazing and torture are endemic to illegitimate power. Elaine Scarry, in her book *The Body in Pain,* wrote, "In torture, it is in part the obsessive display of agency that permits one person's body to be translated into another person's voice, that allows real human pain to be converted into a regime's fiction of power." Torture occurs when power is uncertain and illegitimate, when a regime is unstable and weak. Here is one possible narrative for this emblem of the Occupation:

The Iraqi people are the exotic, mysterious Other, but also ridiculous figures of fun. We came to liberate them from their primitive state, to modernize and electrify them. But they don't understand, so we must keep them in the dark until the process is complete. We've put them up on a pedestal (the same pedestal we pulled Saddam off of), but this pedestal is made of cardboard, and if they fall off and get modernized (electrified) too soon, they will be killed. They just don't understand. Can't they see that we've occupied them in order to make them free, and that we may have to destroy them in order to save them?

Note: Top military officials now say that the interrogations at Abu Ghraib yielded almost no new intelligence, and that most of the prisoners tortured by the Americans at Abu Ghraib were not linked to the insurgency. Another report said 70–80 percent of the Iraqi detainees at Abu Ghraib were innocents swept up in raids. Tech-niques and procedures designed for "high value terrorist targets" (in Afghanistan and Guantanamo) ended up being used on "cab-drivers, brothers-in-law, and people pulled off the streets." The hooded prisoner being forced to masturbate in front of Lynndie England is named Hayder Sabbar Abd, and he was picked up for "getting out of a cab in a suspicious manner."

1. Nina Bernstein, "Once Tortured, Now Tormented by Photos," *The New York Times,* May 15, 2004.

The preceding lecture was first given, accompanied by 100 projected slides, on June 17, 2004, at the Los Angeles Times Media Center, at the invitation of the Art Center College of Design, and again on July 2, 2004 at Bard College in Annandale-on-Hudson, New York. It is dedicated to my friend Leon Golub, who died on August 8, 2004, in New York City.

9.

Abu Ghraib and the Magic of Images

Charles Stein

> And Earth had lost another portion of the infinite!
> —*America: A Prophecy,* William Blake

This piece will neither begin nor end. In spite of appearances, apocalyptic events are like that. "Now for the first time in history." But it is an eternal incursion that sets all watches new. Writing itself is like that. It waits upon an incursion to gather the thoughts that swarm about it. The thoughts neither begin nor end. But the images of Abu Ghraib that burst upon us last spring, as the images of the planes striking the two towers, seem incursions with their own matter, their own weight, hurtling the realities they carry and that carry them, through the barriers of consciousness, at once unreadable and too readable, setting the mind in motion, ever-once-again attempting to integrate the incommensurable.... Magic is like that. It neither begins nor ends. It casts its images upon a field that it composes.

Historian Ioan P. Couliano[1] indicates that what the Renaissance theory of magic handled under the head of the *phantasmatic* (in the thought of Giordana Bruno, say) becomes divided in the modern world between political persuasion, advertising, and the psychology of eros.

I don't know what magic is, but that it is something fearsome, that it has its darkest patches, that it overwhelms good sense, and that it revels in images.

The phantasmatic is the economy of images. For the magician there was a substance, the *pneuma,* that cosmos and person held in common. ("Pneuma" is Greek for spirit or breath. The Stoics deployed this ordinary term to indicate a special substance common to the individual soul and the universe at large. On it images travel, and, because of it, commerce between the individual person and a more common space is possible.) The pneuma receives and processes *phantasmata:* images emanated by persons and things. The soul receives the influence of the stars because the astral substance was thought to be pneumatic too. Phantasmata are the stuff of eros: by means of them the image of one person can enter the being of another and take possession of their will. Or, indeed, images can replace one's very being. Couliano writes: "The phantasm that monopolizes the soul is the image of an object. Now, since man is soul, and soul is totally occupied by a phantasm, the phantasm is henceforth the soul. It follows that the subject, bereft of his soul, is no longer a subject: the phantasmatic vampire has devoured it internally."[2]

In general, images flow from entities and enter the eye. They pass along internal conduits until the ventricles of the brain receive and process them. They, and the pneumatic substance on which they travel, supply the media by which magical intentions and intensities transmit. Magic is the erotology of the image. Manipulation and desire are its mundane fields of play.

Modern science arose as a set of practices that define the magical by exclusion. Science lives where magic is not; though, interestingly, the converse is less clear: whereas science cannot countenance magic as a serious ontological region, magic has little difficulty finding in scientific practice fit tools for its arsenal. Be that as it may, science proceeds by putting magic to rest. Thus, the manipulations of reality performed through the configurations of the phantasmata and their pneumatic vehicle were supplanted by various methodologies appropriate to several domains— politics, advertising, and erotic psychology, as mentioned above.

Information

Begin with image as information etched in light: its essence is no longer light at all. Light itself is but a stage in information's passaging. Flashed around the Internet, its positions as printout or presence on a computer screen are but transitory moments in the image's problematic identity.

But what of the Abu Ghraib pictures in the face of all of this? These strange, perfectly composed cross-sections of horror, like amateur porn shots, "the real thing"—as if you could "click on it" and have the whole action: the howls of the victims, or their moribund silence; the jeers of the guards, or the business-as-usual shuffling of persons on the prison staff who just happen to be milling around; or the perfectly professional demeanor of the "dog handler."

Consider that the transmission of the Abu Ghraib images flow from the largely unexamined ontological space of the public internet to the private video screen, and you will see immediately where I am going. The video image grasps the psychic pneuma more immediately than the photograph. It enters the "soul" by a certain effluence of information that is more physically palpable than the reflection of image from page of print or emulsion. Electrons from the older screens and sheaves of incident light from the newer ones imprint images on the retina with a certain viscosity, a certain tactility. Thus, if I make an exposure with my digital camera and hurl its information across the Internet to your video screen and thence into your eye, I may be performing a gesture that magicians of old only dreamed of.[3]

But video screens tune in to a domain that crosses national and cultural boundaries, rendering common the psychic emission and reception of images by the ever-growing multitudes that have access to them. Images propelled for political, commercial, and erotic purposes, and images sent from friends or relations, now flash across the same electronic circuits, sharing the same forms of point-and-click receptivity. Thus reunited, they are reacquiring, through technical means, the phantasmatic functions of a pre-modern, magical cosmos.

It should be clear, however, that, ontologically considered, these functions were never truly divided. We do not routinely remind ourselves that the physicalist ontology that governs and limits the technological does not at all comprehend the nature of consciousness itself; but surely we cannot know what an image is apart from such comprehension. How the phantasmatic functions in our being and in the being of the cosmos is not finally controlled by the thinking that, until now, has effected its division into the political, the commercial, and the erotic. The subject of the reunification of the phantasmatic function is therefore certainly on our agenda if we are to grapple with the import of the Abu Ghraib images, their peculiar immediacy and charge. It is quite as if the pneuma of the old magical theory were being reconfigured before and within our fascinated gaze.

A part of this reconfiguration has to do with how our

use of images is changing as the technology of images changes. It seems that we now take place within a world-wide culture that allows us to obsess and delight in the discovery of our own being through video images that we retrieve from the air and flash across the internet to friends and relatives, or store for immediate auto-delectation. In such a context *the image document* has primary ontological status. Representation and thing represented collapse into each other and coincide. How the image serves as evidence for another reality than its own electronic immediacy is a matter for negotiation and interpretation. But to manipulate the image is to manipulate the self. To make an image of another under conditions of violent restraint is to engage a magical efficacy of the darkest water.

The primacy or autonomy of the image has clearly been observable in advertising, politics, and erotology for as long as images have circulated through public media, but the immediacy of the transformation of the image fact into public force is something new. It is this immediacy that calls or recalls into configuration the magical pneuma. Image strikes reality with a swiftness and acuity that reality cannot correct or resist but can only confirm and sustain. And this is true not only where the image is newsworthy broadcast material of a conventionally public event. It is just as true for a snapshot, or, as in the case of Abu Ghraib, the documentation of private acts as image trophies. The private is public by virtue of the common media by which the images of both are constituted. And when a private image finds itself caught in a web of global import, its dark magic may well work its way into the pneuma, that is, the collective soul of the world and, through that, into the destiny of nations.

The Abu Ghraib images, indeed, piggy-back on their position in a global configuration that made their publicity an instantaneously universal acquisition. Everybody knows them. The entire world (that is, the world not immediately under the heel of the American military yet subject to its economic hegemony) already felt every gesture of the occupation of Iraq as legible and relevant. But with the release of the images, the predatory character of American will, long in formation in the global imagination, has taken definitive pictorial shape.

In America, of course, the images are subject to a different series of transformations, of exposures and suppressions ... suppressed as military secret, leaked as part of the still partially clandestine struggle between governmental bureaus, posted on front pages and news shows as exposé, but also flashed as gleeful breakout of nocturnal pornographic image forms into the daylight of the "news-day" for all to see—on newsstands for an instant, a splash on the surface of urban consciousness. ("Did you see them?" "Yes I saw them. I wanted to look away, but I saw them.")

In the U.S., the suppression of visual information regarding America's military operations has been in effect since the first Gulf War and its invisible 100,000 slaughtered Iraqis. We have seen no images of the million and half children and adults lost to disease and hunger during the "sanctions," and none of the current Mesopotamian holocaust. This suppression of imagery has surely produced a hugely charged though empty, domestic "image space," if I can quickly invent a concept.

In addition to this, consider the focus of the Abu Ghraib images on the human body in attitudes of what would be the very archetypes of abjection were it not for the fact that the circumstance itself causes *instance* to precede and override *archetype.* Nothing is left for the symbolical imagination to elaborate. You are presented with the literal fact of the image and what it represents, fully "read," saturated with meaning, and, at the same time, eerily intimate, cold, and, I want to say, transcendentally illegible.

Something is accumulating in these images, quite as if they were ancient portraits of an impossible humanity; the concentrated horror of the phenomena themselves, projecting violently into the information that light carries—the events in no way *essentially* informational—but thrown adventitiously into the light that transmits them—that MAN, that MAN, that MAN, under the weight of an unending regression and darkness, at the edge of the concrete character of the real itself, not modified, not integrated, not contextualized, not KNOWN—overwhelming its own representation—that HEAD on that BODY, on tiptoes, by command, or fallen on the stinking prison floor. Or that thumbs-up grin of sexy guard girl—the accomplishment of a sarcastically degenderized military—leering over a bagged and processed corpse; and that other gestureless, faceless creature, standing there, leash in hand, while a mass of prime matter, hairy and not yet insensate—the very "image" of sentience itself—lugs its weight almost out of the eyeshot of its indifferent captors, dumped by its cage.

In the public sphere, imagery has always been wielded for power—to coerce or induce action, political or mercantile. But the Abu Ghraib images seem to be out of control—at once snap shot, espionage, blackmail, pornography—at once representation and emergence of the thing itself. They seem to lay open a wound in the "astral plane," whose "lower vibrations" have always been the denizens of lust, sadism, torture, and, in general, a dark economy housing partially differentiated agencies and the urgencies of disordered power. This quasi-metaphysical disorder feeds on the disorder of the physical situation in which it arose. The chaos of Abu Ghraib—the filth, the inappropriate staffing, the overcrowding, the daily subjection to bombardment, the rat- and insect-infested food—surely contributes to the underlying darkness of the situation and, even if not depicted there, is subliminally registered in the images themselves.

And it is finally the images that, in bearing (say it!) a demonic charge, are the site of the demonic itself. Representation and thing represented coincide, particularly here where the represented thing (torture as practiced in a contemporary American prison) has been so utterly repressed that many of us, upon seeing these images, felt that we couldn't see what they were at all. The testimony to the contrary of black Americans, for whom the reality of prison torture and racist abuse is familiar indeed, shows a major split in the psychic reality of the races in this country and provides qualifying detail regarding the "image space" and its dynamic characteristics that I hazarded a moment ago. Different regions of that image space—one might say different vicinities in the public pneuma—are differently charged, differently potentiated, relative to different populations and their experiences.[4]

In Iraq and throughout the Arab world, the images, banned as such by orthodox Islam, are distributed to disclose the true character of the American occupation, to stimulate resistance / resurgence, but also to awaken approbation for the more severe imprecations of the Moslem faith and thus to stimulate "Coalition" outrage at the Arab Press for propagating the images and creating disorder. (As I write, [August 8, 2004] I learn that Al Jazeera has been silenced in Baghdad by the American puppet, Allawi.)

The image space in the Arab world, of course, has its own dynamical characteristics, not the least of which is a general interdiction on representational imagery—an interdiction that it shares with the main line of Orthodox Judaism. The sentiment behind this interdiction shows a cultural sensitivity to the magical pneuma and an attempt to control magic by a total elimination of its most salient means.

For Islam in general, the trichotomization of the phantasmatic may not have occurred at all, or may have done so only partially. Couliano sees that the magical ontology that Giordano Bruno develops late in the European Renaissance has features delivered to it from Medieval Islamic culture, features that by no means have passed away in modern Islam, whose resistance to the West is as much that of a surviving high culture as it is the expression of its fundamentalist wing—a high culture for whom the magical pneuma and the necessity of its suppression have an urgency that the culture of the West can little appreciate or understand. And yet the "image space" into which the Abu Ghraib images have fallen and which they have so powerfully reactivated is, in spite of these vast differences, now, a common one.

. . . Back in America, remember that the prelude to the Abu Ghraib images was the "scandal" of the leaked photos of flag-draped coffins, "and now this!"

Now nothing. The day of wanton images subsides into the most arcane legal wrangling about the technical definition of torture. Imagine: two lawyers standing in a hall at Abu Ghraib, while a naked animal cringes in his offal. They are discussing just which strokes and lashes, hoods and probes and positions are licit instruments for extracting vital information ("the ticking bomb defense") from one of the pieces of dirt the indiscriminate steam-shovel of "intelligence" has scarfed up from the random streets of Sadr City to wring out for secrets only to dump them back again if still alive—if female, to be murdered by her very family for the shame of her submission; if male forever emasculated and diminished before his world.

Violated religious feeling, sexual exposure, inexculpable shame, impotent outrage, betrayal, a sense that the worst fears of minds most generous towards the American "liberators" had come true, must swarm like gnats around these pictures, charging them with a fury that we in our incomprehension can still pick up through their very forms: that naked man on a leash knocked over besides his cage, those hooded ikons.

The first Abu Ghraib image I saw was the one with Lyndie England holding that man on a leash, humanity irrelevant, physical, fallen by his cage. If nothing else, the world of images performs magic on the world of images. For me, a thousand images of abject humanity were sucked up and expunged by this one. Only certain drawings of Goya—but suddenly, an understanding of those uncanny late Philip Guston hooded creatures with the cigarettes—withstand. (Guston's hooded figures always suggested Ku Klux Klan members, but the hoods on victims in the Abu Ghraib pictures reverse the sense of Guston's cartoons, increasing, retrospectively, their uncanny quality.)

Where and when exactly are we?—do we pretend to perch in some Celestial Academy of Kabbalistic justice when we contemplate such matters as the staggering stupidity of the American response to the terrorist response to America's world-wide staggering stupidity—when we think to respond to the Abu Ghraib images?

If there is no Academy on High, perhaps there is one still meeting in dens and caves, still watching for snakes and tigers, still ready for beheadings by blue goddesses with beautiful blood-hungry eyes. The images of the *tantrikas,* however, are set to test our consciousness: to strengthen awareness before a terror that, for us, is limited by the possibility of our own demise. But the horror and menace of these images strike at our very humanity, or, if we identify with our country, break the very spirit of national honor. Something more than tantric presence of mind would be required to transmute what is registered there.

The business of magic in the end is to compel ontology: to force what is in us to awaken to the ontological force of what we are. If an image can vampirize the soul, it is here in the soul's conviction of the real that it does its work. It has always been the case that the only antidote to the magic of an image is the magic of passing beyond all image, that is, beyond magic itself. If the Abu Ghraib images surpass in darkness and efficacy all images before, can it be that they herald some unheard of soteriological possibility? But where the soul at stake is not that of an individual but of a nation ...

The Shadow

One doesn't have to be a Jungian to appreciate Jung's reflections on what he calls the "Shadow" and its phenomenology: that the psychic growth of the individual or of a collective like a nation depends upon an awakening to the images of evil with which the soul, individual or collective, is resonant: not only that each of us is capable of the whole gamut of viciousness that contemporary event makes hideously manifest, but that in the failure to experience the fullness of our nature, we project what we deny and enter upon struggles with others that are truly struggles within ourselves. Can we doubt that the images of Abu Ghraib have opened a new phase in the reality of these phenomena?

Hear, then, "the many minds of the Shadow" as they find themselves *into* the Abu Ghraib images:

1. The brute materiality of my somatic existence renders me susceptible to torture: unendurable positions, probings, beatings, electrostimulations: My bodily pain is my most intimate state, and in its extremity it is utterly universal and anonymous.

2. Our physical vulnerability renders us ineluctably susceptible to shame: the brutal words of our tormentors meld our physical vulnerability into a palpable sense of moral depravity: we are what we are made to feel, are what we are made to seem, are what we are named by those who despise us or ignore us in our misery.

3. We ourselves are these tormentors. We too need to obey our commanders, to perform adequately in their eyes, to

transcend our merely personal sensibilities so as to be able to perform the brutal deeds our country, in its need, demands that we perform. To be who we are—the protagonists in an international drama where there is only terror on every side—we must overcome our squeamishness, our consciences, our fear. Only our abjection corresponds to our edification; only our will to destroy and punish the evil of our enemy guarantees our elevation above him.

4. Our fear and our boredom, our discomfiture, our camaraderie—our identification with our fellows—we are all in the same boat, all able to endure the brutality we suffer at the hands of our commanders, from the virulence of the enemy, from the cruel conditions of nature itself—only by accepting the terms of our servitude, of our duty to the ikons of country, democracy, freedom ...

5. We too are these commanders—we see the Big Picture, the cause of the benevolent empire, the work of God, the impossibility of retreat, the necessity of preserving the chain of command. Or we too are utterly compromised, slowly having abandoned all commitment to truth or conscience, having given ourselves over to sadistic ecstasies, having come up through the ranks and endured whatever brutalities, whatever seductions by the thrill of

power, the habits of avarice, the alienation from the creative life within us, the need to stave off our own smallness, vulnerability, and self-doubt through the pleasures of rank and command.

6. We too are the callous witness; the implacable eye; the quality of divine detachment that because it IS divine, authentically atemporal, beyond all suffering, all abjection, all need—can BE the implacable universal eye of information—can Be Being reduced to information, Being reduced to the state of a pure witness, the ancient camera flashing what goes down across the internets of eternity without compassion or fear of consequence or the susceptibility of interestedness of any kind.

The moral matrix into which all of this dissolves cannot arise in Being without an awakening that passes through these states and, no doubt, infinitely more besides. But it is the very intensity of these images and the thoroughness and pitiless depravity with which they call upon our Shadow that the possibility of an awakening of a commensurate intensity depends. If the images and their dark magic, however, pertain in the end not to individual conscience but to the spiritual vitality of a nation, it is doubtful that any such transformation is in the offing.

America A Prophecy

On a global scale, it is an image that sustains a possibility, and certain images seem, for a time, to sustain Possibility itself. The institution of such images is a mystery, as is their downfall. The geniuses of Madison Avenue might work at it, the spin doctors in their think tanks or offices as well, but even they know that they work with probabilities alone and cannot fathom when or how they will succeed or fail. It is not every day that an image ruins a nation, but these tortured images have proclaimed a great divide in the history of the United States, a moment when a sustaining idealism sustains no more. It was an idealism that had weathered every chastening revelation, every call to conscience: slavery, the subjugation of women, the atrocities of Dresden, Tokyo, Hiroshima, Vietnam, East Timor, rebounding *qua* idealism as something living within the collective soul precisely as other than the facts of the matter, riding above the facts of the matter as the spirit of possibility, the Goddess Possibility, under the name of America. With the Abu Ghraib images—and I mean the images, not the facts—because the facts are no more true of Abu Ghraib than of the hundreds of imageless American prisons, the hidden dungeons of Tadjikistan or wherever they are around the American world—but the advent of the images have dealt a death blow to the Goddess Possibility in her American incarnation. That incarnation is no more. The United States can never again don that mask. It is finished. And it was these images (and the reconstituted pneumatic space of their distribution) that brought her down.

1. Ioan. P. Couliano. *Eros and Magic in the Renaissance* (Chicago: University of Chicago Press, 1987.

2. Ibid. p. 31.

3. This only *seems* to contradict the common observation that viewing a video screen or computer monitor suppresses somatic consciousness, that we become disembodied zomboid awarenesses when our gaze is thus absorbed. But consider how this occurs. With video, the eye is captivated by incident rather than reflected light and by the subliminal movement of the raster process: the lightening fast inscribing of the image across the screen by infinitesimal dots and lines. This makes its impact upon the eye far more complexly and violently than an emulsion or print-based image where the picture is delivered by milder, reflected light and doesn't involve anything like the raster dynamic. The hyper-involvement in the video image is suppressed as one becomes engaged with image content, so, in effect, a greater part of one's somatic being is simply put out of play, i.e. rendered unconscious in order to sustain identification with what occurs on the screen.

4. Couliano's remark that, for magical theory, the soul itself is so close to being an image that it can be replaced by one, perhaps makes it possible to grasp the magical efficacy of the Abu

Ghraib images by reading them into a Lacanian perspective. Lacan took an interest in the phenomena of Courtly Love in his late seminar *Encore,* and, of course, it is in Courtly Love that the magical concept of the image has its most vivid instance, i.e. the fascinating image of the beloved enters the soul of the lover and renders it incapable of functioning in any way but oriented toward her.

Lacanians connect image and language by observing the relation between Lacan's early conception of the "Stadium of the Mirror" and the formation of the ego as the subject of discourse. The infant becomes an ego at the moment when she sees herself in a mirror as the object of her mother's gaze. Similarly, the swarming universe of speakers encroaches upon the infant and awakens her desire to speak. In both cases, the ego is formed externally: the person assumes a place in a world that exists before her. The ego in itself is a blank, a cipher, a lack, that is filled by an image or a signifier.

In the application of Lacanian theory to cinema and art, the process by which the viewer comes to identify (spontaneously and subliminally) with an image is related to this originary emptiness: the emptiness is filled by the hero or heroine of the film or the subject of the photograph or portrait.

Now consider the Abu Ghraib images. Where can the viewer's ego rest in an identification with the image? The tortured victim. But a spontaneous recoil accompanies the spontaneous attempt of the ego to locate itself in this way. It is simply too horrible, too demeaning. The torturer? Again, the series of images of these people is too morally distressing, too unacceptable to allow identification. Finally, there is the eye of the camera, the field of consciousness that includes both torturer and victim. But again, the complicity of the camera in the act of torture even to the point of being part of the torture apparatus itself eliminates this option. In short, the identification cannot stabilize: the point of identification circulates virulently among the positions and will not come to rest.

While this analysis jibes with the responses of sensitive liberals and much of the American population, it requires comment regarding American Blacks, Arabs in general, and those Americans whose political attitudes are formed or confirmed by Rush Limbaugh and his ilk. Clearly Arabs and Blacks may indeed identify with the torture victims, and the demented followers of "Rush," for whom the Abu Ghraib pictures look like college hazing pranks, seem to have little difficulty identifying with the torturers. Interestingly, Donald Rumsfeld's initial reaction to the pictures before the Senate Foreign Relations Committee was like that of most of us, not like his demented constituency. This does not show him as a man of conscience, particularly, but only that the structure of his ego refuses to locate itself in the position of the torturer in spite of his own role in allowing the conditions of Abu Ghraib to develop and his apparently having given the orders to turn the torture screws up a notch.

10.
Abu Ghraib: A Howl

Richard Grossinger

1.

The images were iconic the moment they arrived. Indelible. They radiated the meta-historical chill of 9/11—that history itself was turning on a dime.

They not only had the glow of a newly-discovered cache of malignant Rembrandts, each one special in a dreaded way, but were a "Wanted" poster of our furtive crimes, an interred body disturbed in its crypt.

At the same time, they were as absolute and remote as a robot's view of rocks strewn across a Martian desert or a cyclonic pattern on Neptune. Their clarity, arid and inviolate, suggests something even rarer: a photograph taken and recovered from inside a dream, from inside a collective dreaming.

They shouldn't exist at all. Photos are rarely taken inside dreams, never smuggled out.

The soldiers, assorted contractors, and mercenaries who chronicled their revels with videocams were agents of a ritual force. Just as the orders to carry out torture and humiliation came down to them along a military chain of command, the inexplicable impulse to document them came down another command like a fog of war (see Homer's *Iliad*), from unseen tricksters and ghosts who, since the birth of consciousness, have duped humans into enacting what they otherwise least intend. (Unless, of course, they came down the same military chain with the explicit goal of blackmail.)

Amateur, adolescent, vulgar, conceited, horrific, irresistible, the portraits are luminous records, confessions of sacred sins—a devil's tarot, one by one by one by one, from a medieval forge, rendered deceptively modern and ordinary by digital technology.

Tarots are pools in which not only landscapes and figures but aliases form. Tarots write fortunes in the most profound and incriminating sense. Their characters cannot be dismissed, because they are not human; their landscapes cannot be evaded, because they comprise domains and their opposites.

Minting tarots is a trademark of our Babylonian occupation: witness the tasteless playing cards issued to represent foes of the so-called coalition of the willing—a threat-display of gloating and dissing the enemy as well as a surrogate taking of scalps (by men in business suits, no less). Yet the neocons couldn't distribute a Baath deck without its archetypal other manifesting too: a Bush Administration gallery of knaves (Rummy, Cheney, Condi, W. himself) mirroring the Iraqi hunted, card by card.

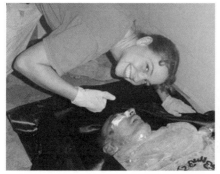

As much as the Administration and its apologists want to absolve themselves of blame and minimize the acts, reality cannot be changed. George W.'s dissociation and lukewarm apology mean nothing. He can yammer until he is blue in the face and talking in tongues, about how the majority of our soldiers are good people who intend well, how Americans are decent at core, how we came to Iraq to liberate Iraqis from a horrific despot, etc., etc. But those on the ground see our real agenda. America is broadcast planetwide on satellite, demonstrated firsthand by our corporate offices and occupying forces. From Asia to Africa to Chile and Peru, those outside our gestalt have gawked at our action cinema and been condescended to by our ads and franchise outlets. Soon enough they will watch Michael Moore's *F 9/11* in which American troops fire mortar after mortar at Iraqi housing while the high-decibel, earphoned shriek of "Burn, motherfucker, burn!" numbs their minds. After that they or other troops will grope and tease the genitals of their hooded captives.

The images will always speak louder, will have a charisma and impact W. can only dream of. Say what he wants, people will judge us by our actions, not his words. In fact, his words are a grotesque façade.

What did he say anyway: that just because Americans did these things doesn't mean they do things like that? Pretty pathetic. More than half the Iraqi people, in a poll taken three months later, had no trouble voting to the contrary.

The effigies from Abu Ghraib brand every heedless lie of this Administration, from the disenfranchisement of voters of color in Florida to the trumped-up evidence about weapons of mass destruction, from the accomplicing of Saddam for 9/11 to the rounding-up of innocents on the streets of Baghdad (while claiming that they were Baath dead-enders and terrorists) and the annihilation of freedom fighters in Fallujah (while claiming they were foreign terrorists).

In truth, the cadres who commandeered planes on 9/11 and flew them into buildings were hardly the ones that American soldiers snatched from their homes and off the streets, stripped, and forced to masturbate and give blow jobs—but the slippage, the iconography of Abu Ghraib took one into another, so that all the bodies, beneath robes and hoods, became the same body. Bush and Cheney wanted that mistake to be made, wanted us to believe that we could get retribution for the World Trade Center and Pentagon by conscripting Iraqi proxies, removing their clothes, and exposing them as wimps when tortured, by proving they had vulnerable bodies just like everyone else. Our "leaders" won't admit it, and they quite possibly didn't even tell themselves, but they knew exactly what kind of sadomasochistic improvisation was likely to follow.

The perpetrators have turned nudity into obscenity and projected their own guiltily stolen pleasures and thralldoms onto everyone. Naked flesh as sacrament is debased, the body as ikon mutilated, converted into the body as torture. Of course, it was the body of Christ they were martyring too, but they forgot that.

The images are us. Look at them and you will see America—the pornography, sadism, hyper-sexualization, hazing, incarceration, recreational racism, and ritual violence of everyday patriotic life here. Abu Ghraib expresses the banality of reality TV alongside the apathetic lust of boys' (and girls') night out. Americans support a ten-billion-dollar-a-year porn industry churning out videos that foreshadow Abu Ghraib in their storyline, their callousness and abuse of the marginal and helpless. Businessmen, politicians, and the general *hoi polloi* head for Vegas to stare numbly at mock bondage and other harbingers of recreational military torture. And yet we are surprised when unsupervised soldiers round up foreigners and deploy them in ritual turpitude, hostages who by their cultural styles and resistance to Americanization arouse the homoerotic homophobia and terror the invaders are already experiencing?

Everything that is tawdry and vapid about George W. Bush's polity is somewhere in the Abu Ghraib reliquary—Donald Trump, NASCAR, Paris Hilton, Enron, Mel Gibson's slasher version of the crucifixion (church groups invited after prayer), the bludgeoning of transsexuals (Eddie/Gwen Araujo cum Teena Brandon), *Playboy* and *Hustler* (sorry, Hugh and Larry, you can have the First Amendment and artistic freedom but not the moral high ground too), bombs at abortion clinics, gang initiations, the Tyson Perdue execution line, pig and cow dismemberment machines, ducks and geese hatched in tiny boxes and bloated for canapés, the controlled science of lethal injection, electric chairs (their picketing advocates crooning "Happy Trails" on execution days), the ritual jailing of drug addicts, lynchings as bonding ceremonies, the salacious quest for a snuff film, corporate fraud so rampant it is taken for granted, Haliburton's obscene profits, the daily swagger of blue-collar bullies and road rage, gun-toting fifteen-year-olds seeking revenge over slights in the playground, the titillating voyeurism of the suburban mall. Humvees, supersize-me ... look carefully at the photographs and you will see snapshots of all the aspects of American life bristling through their oblivious, trite surfaces like poltergeists on truth serum. That's what's so brilliant about the Abu Ghraib debacle. It discloses the shadow of America, the dark side of unfettered liberty and the pursuit of happiness. It tells the world what, despite our best intentions, Iraq and the rest of humanity will become if we naively globalize our culture as the great democratizing engine. Abu Ghraib is the omen that we cannot export mere freedom of speech and free markets without a healthy culture and compassionate, mature citizens backing them.

If you look more closely at Abu Ghraib, you will see Donald Rumsfeld embracing Saddam Hussein, signing off on the brutal invasion of Iran, "Go kill those bastards"; later excusing the gassing of the Kurds because he was "our thug" then; the CIA arming Osama and bankrolling pre-Taliban militia. The Vice-President's routine greed and cruelty (and barely suppressed scurrility) are a mere layer below his surface. Do you think he is innocent of Abu Ghraib? The pictures show

Paul Wolfowitz forgetting how many American troops have already been killed, because without Paul Wolfowitz and Richard Cheney, without their sociopathic idealisms and embittered disregard for the suffering of others, these pictures could not have been taken. The deeper landscapes of Abu Ghraib look more like these guys than their own staged portraits do. And they cannot run from spirit photography.

Rush Limbaugh got it right when he said Abu Ghraib was no worse than frat night out—this is a party-boy administration. Discarding the Geneva Convention on prisoners of war is the same act of careless self-enfranchisement as tossing out environmental laws for campaign contributors or lewdly scaring the hell out of the pledges. It is Good Old Boy fun turned dark and ugly. It is Privilege, freed of decades of restraint, feigning the imprimatur of God. It is what happens when incompletely rehabilitated alcoholics (with an evangelical constituency) connive crocodile diplomacy and take over the engines of war.

The gallery at Abu Ghraib foreshadows as well the tragic fate of the "good apples," the brave Americans who believed and defended us unconditionally, who gave their bodies and lives because they honored the flag and the Constitution. The images reveal through a glass darkly Bush-Cheney's exploitation of those young men and women's innocence and sense of duty, in the face of the ultimate sacrifice. The

Administration golems (sans Mr. Powell) care about as much for our solders as they do for the melting glaciers and endangered species and carcinogens released into rivers. They take it all as their entitlement.

Don't kid yourself about a bunch of girls and guys from Appalachia (or Queens or Kansas) letting off steam. Did you really think that these were Lynndie England's stillborn fantasies and inner life? Behind Abu Ghraib stands famous nice guy George W. Bush, hazing king of the Skull & Bones, closet sadist supreme, nodding with a deceitful wink when Rummy asks him if it's okay to do an end around Geneva at Gitmo, the Sunni triangle (another wink), and throughout the Taliban west (a plausibly deniable nod). We see W. letting out his blood-curdling whoop as the attack on Baghdad begins. We see Dick Cheney drunk and raising mayhem on his Yale dorm floor before dropping out and heading for Wyoming; we see him clearing the way for Haliburton; we see him pretending to be sober and responsible and megapatriotic while savoring his international scofflaw status, snickering to Prince Bander Bush, "Saddam is toast!" And you are surprised by the scandal at Abu Ghraib?

Here too are after-images of Ronald Reagan dispatching death squads into the wretched villages of El Salvador and Guatemala, turning the insane from the hospitals onto the streets, pretending not to know the word "AIDS." His amnesia at death was the amnesia he lived by, the selective memory whereby a movie was as good as the real thing. Ronald Reagan posturing before the Berlin Wall, pretending to end Communism, is emblematically present at Abu Ghraib. He didn't murder or rape anyone or destroy villages with his own hands, but he turned a magnificently tuned deaf ear and blind eye while allowing, in fact encouraging, mayhem and torture to be carried out on his watch. George W. has cultivated the same strategic Alzheimer's, pretending not to see, pretending not to hear, pretending to be a soldier, but imperiously skipping the only war in which he could have fought.

The Abu Ghraib photographs expose the abuses and depredations underwritten by the Reagan-Bush cabal. They show that what we call freedom and democracy is something far more insidious. When we build prisons and weapon systems as rapidly as classrooms and churn out cop-killing video games and sell goods by semblances of women's bodies (while pretending to decry and punish vice), we are creating a moral double standard, a schizophrenia that must inevitably lead to post-moral stasis and an ethical vacuum. When slaughterhouse workers in West Virginia are filmed stomping on live chickens for fun, flinging them against the wall, strangling them with latex gloves while hamming it up, squeezing birds till they explode, and ripping off their heads for a pen to leave graffiti in blood, how far are we from hell itself? How can we expect our minions to act any differently from their country cousins? Why wouldn't the same arrogant, sociopathic treatment of objectified bodies be transferred from commercial fowl to commercial prisoners of war? The secret taping of the slaughterhouse episodes was in fact sarcastically called "Kentucky Fried Chicken's Abu Ghraib." But the metonymy is backwards: the institutionalization of our disrespect for animals and contempt for life came first (don't kid yourself about Right to Life; most of the ad-libbing executioners on the meat assembly lines were self-proclaimed anti-abortion born-agains). The deprecating humor of the journalist who thought up the name "KFC's Abu Ghraib" shows that we still don't understand who we are and what Abu Ghraib says about us; we still don't take our acts seriously. We don't realize that we are what we do, what we eat, how we play, how we treat those who are most helpless and in our care, in need of our protection. What we find amusing or entertaining in a slaughterhouse or striptease will set the ultimate moral bar for our soldiers ("ultimate" because, while only a few committed atrocities, an entire nation was implicated).

Abu Ghraib is the ineluctable product of the squalid American prison industry, for which it was a vintage road show—

the effusion of what goes on in prisons throughout the United States for our growing constituency of incarcerated people, mostly African American and Hispanic, every minute, every hour. As we pull more and more harmless people off our own streets for fabricated and convenient crimes and hire more and more sadists and molesters posing as constabularies and priests to chastise them at their own pleasure, we engender blowback, release creatures beyond our wildest imagination. America is the only country in the world identifying throwaway humans and turning them into "materials" for an incarceration machine (we already have more African American youth in jails than colleges). Right-to-lifers beware: investors have gone into serious competition with God (none of this abortion-clinic righteousness)—they are now laying claim to the cell and fetus, the labor of poor families; they deal directly in bodies and souls, from juvenile arrests and solitary confinement to the living death of Three Strikes and fixed sentencing, from an international commerce in organs to Death Row itself, generating profit at every stage (a minimum of $73,000 now for prison guards in California, more than primary- and secondary-school teachers because, after all, we must recruit the best and the brightest for our institutions of learning).

Where do you think the curriculum of Abu Ghraib was written? Where do you think the military found Charles

Graner, Jr.? He was a bona fide irregular regulator of bodies in the domestic prison bureaucracy, a practiced torturer. So he was exported by the Administration along with all his and their assumptions underlying a growth industry of lock-up and deprivation of all rights for ever-expanding crimes of desire and poverty. In the same way that the neocons are so tunnel-visioned they don't get the obvious iconography of a huge African population in chains and booming concentration-camp construction along with the continuous reinvention of punishment, they provincially ship its whole mechanism intact to Guantanamo, Kandahar, Baghdad, Najaf, and Tikrit and begin harvesting local product for storage and interrogation.

George W. was benighted enough to proclaim tearing down Abu Ghraib as an act of atonement and collateral on good deeds. It is not even an act of recognition, let alone of reconciliation. He might start with acknowledging the Abu Ghraibization of the American landscape, from penitentiaries on Adirondack lakes to San Quentin, with emphasis on his own beloved Texasylum and posses along the Border. He might also tell the prisoners of the American military the crimes they are charged with, the evidence on which those crimes are based, and read them something like their Miranda rights.

2.

Capitalist appropriation, facile wealth, pre-teen sex, corporate cocktail parties, suburban swinging, and reckless fun are what America is about, what we are exporting. Is it any wonder that Islamic mullahs and ayatollahs (to say nothing of madrasa-trained militants) hold the ears of their people? In which country would you rather raise a daughter? The answer is not quite as much a no-brainer as you might think. Yes, America, for sure. No one wants a child stoned to death for not being a virgin on her marriage day. But would you rather have a teen girl invisible in a chador, or with tongue piercings, ritually vomiting, on the street, paying the rent by doing tricks, performing in the porn business? Would you prefer a patriarch or a pimp? As stifling and primitive as those societies are—misogynous, violent, revengeful—they do not seduce their youth with the spoils of false progressivism or minimize the initiation mystery of life and death; they do not play everyone for the fool the way America does. Few Western women would want to grow up in an Islamic fundamentalist culture (though Nadine Gordimer's *The Pickup* offers an opposing viewpoint); yet why can we not understand the horror of religious Muslims at the prospect of the globalization of America's version of courtship and romance?

Whether or not we are contesting evil at large, we are, as Abu Ghraib proves, fighting both for and against something far more ambiguous, far less morally benign. Of course, the truth is: we are *always* fighting evil, as most peoples on Earth are. Yet evil is far cleverer than we ever are; it knows how to exploit our benightedness and gullibility, how to lure us onto its turf. Abu Ghraib is evil's turning of the tables, its counterpunch. If you make war on evil questionlessly, you will soon enough find yourself committing unanticipated sins, enacting bizarre crimes. A misguided attack on evil that in fact creates evil.

While we may rant about the intolerance of fundamentalist Islam and its incompatibility with liberal democracies, about the clash of civilizations between backward orientalist and progressive Western societies, we overlook a more basic dilemma—that the geopolitico-ideological role of the United States is not innocently progressive; it requires the espionage of Mossad, the investments of the House of Saud and similar royalist regimes, puppet and/or other corrupt military dictatorships throughout the developing world, occupation of indigenous communities, seizure of lands and resources, and the establishment of a transnational chain of Abu Ghraibs (with local management) to stash the most effective native opponents of globalization.

The United States is pretending that the 9/11 attacks

uniquely transcended the total eradication of Hiroshima, the slaughter and exile of Tutsis by Hutus in Rwanda, of indigenous Africans by Muslims in Sudan, of Cambodians by Pol Pot's army, of Kurds by Iraqi Baaths, of East Timorese by Indonesian soldiers, of Mexicans crossing into the U.S. by techno-cops. President Bush acts as though the destruction of the World Trade Center (and part of the Pentagon) are such uniquely horrific acts committed by such evil and craven individuals that they license him to retaliate everywhere with no holds barred, to police the world (that is what he wanted to be able to do in the first place), and to by-pass the U.S. Constitution, the Bill of Rights, and the Geneva Convention, ignoring that the attacks were precisely strikes against the corrupt acts of a self-appointed global policeman, with no cognizance of its own aggressively careless behavior toward either the innocent or the guilty.

Not joining as an equal—an equally vulnerable community—the family of nations inhabiting the Cold War landscape, we have chosen to banish our guilt toward the impoverished peoples that make up most of the planet, a responsibility to which we once paid lip service. By making ourselves look more decent and well-intentioned than we are and by depriving radical Islam of a viable political position, the Administration keeps the pot boiling to everyone's detriment. They would rather hoard wealth, power, and resources than take the first perilous steps toward an equitable and sane world. (How much worse anyway is Islamic fanaticism than Zionist fanaticism, which has Jehovah deeding all of Palestine plus parts of Iraq and Egypt to the Jews, or Christian fanaticism, which for centuries has brutalized, robbed, and enslaved some of the most impoverished and gentlest peoples on Earth?)

At this point it would seem that the sad verdict for the planet is between global capitalism masquerading as liberal democracy and anti-democratic, paternalistic, theocratic fundamentalist fascism—except that the Jihadists are partly a symptom of capitalism's global industrial attack on their homeland.

Just as 9/11 foreshadowed Abu Ghraib, Abu Ghraib's latency made 9/11 inevitable. Before 9/11 we mostly did not understand the nature of the horror that we were inflicting on the poor of the world. 9/11 was informative: "People are pretty angry at us." Since 9/11, Bush and crew have squandered most of the global sympathy for America by pretending that the attacks were unprovoked and by launching an equally ideological and inflatedly moralistic crusade against our supposed enemies. As long as we have a "war on terrorism" under a banner of promoting "human rights," we are doomed not only to miss what it is we are exporting but the essential tyranny that we are imposing on ourselves.

We must not allow al-Qaeda to frame the debate, to spearhead the only effective counter-attack on the corruptions of the capitalist universe; in fact, we can only defeat the terrorists by joining in such an attack; but, in order to do that, we must first realize how their use of "terror" is throwing a mirror up to our own deeds.

The only sensible way to address Abu Ghraib is to recognize it as a symptom of our culture's pathology and try to heal the indulgences and corrupt institutions that underlie it before it is too late. It may be too late already, but we have no alternative.

Abu Ghraib is the warning at the gates to hell, the precursor of where we are headed if we think we can kill or imprison whatever remotely threatens us in this world.

Part 2 of this essay is abridged from a short review of *Welcome to the Desert of the Real* by Slavoj Žižek; the rest of the review appears in a forthcoming book tentatively entitled *On the Integration of Nature: Post-9/11 Biopolitical Notes.*

About the Contributors

Meron Benvenisti was deputy mayor of Jerusalem from 1971 to 1978. Benvenisti is currently a columnist for *Ha'aretz,* Israel's largest newspaper. He is the author of many books, including *Intimate Enemies: Jews and Arabs in a Shared Land* and *City of Stone: The Hidden History of Jerusalem.* Benvenisti lives in Jerusalem.

Mark Danner is a staff writer at *The New Yorker* and regular contributor to *The New York Review of Books.* He is Professor of Journalism at University of California at Berkeley and Henry R. Luce Professor of Human Rights and Journalism at Bard College. Danner writes about foreign affairs and American politics. He divides his time between San Francisco and New York.

Barbara Ehrenreich is a writer, activist, and novelist who appears in publications ranging from *Mother Jones* to *Time.* She is the author of many books including *Blood Rites: Origins and History of the Passions of War* and the recent bestseller, *Nickel and Dimed: On (Not) Getting By in America.*

John Gray is Professor of European Thought at the London School of Economics. He is the author of *Al Qaeda and*

What it Means to be Modern, False Dawn, and *Two Faces of Liberalism.* He lives in London.

Richard Grossinger is an anthropologist and the author of numerous books, including *Planet Medicine, The Night Sky, Out of Babylon,* and *Embryogenesis.*

David Matlin is a novelist, poet, and essayist. He teaches literature and creative writing at San Diego State University. His most recent book, *Prisons: Inside the New America— From Vernooykill Creek to Abu Ghraib* is being published by North Atlantic Books in 2005. Matlin lives in San Diego.

Charles Stein is the author of eleven books of poetry including *The Hat Rack Tree* and the forthcoming *From Mimir's Head* (Station Hill/Barrytown, Ltd); a long-term poetic project, *theforestforthetrees;* translations of Greek epic, philosophical, and Hermetic poetry; a critical study of the poet Charles Olson and his use of the writings of C.G. Jung called *The Black Chrysanthemum* (also from Station Hill Press). He was the editor of *Being = Space x Action,* published by North Atlantic Books.

David Levi Strauss is a writer and critic in New York, where his essays and reviews appear regularly in *Artforum* and

Aperture. He is the author of many works, including his collection of essays on photography and politics, *Between the Eyes,* with an introduction by John Berger; *The Book of 101 Books: Seminal Photography Books of the Twentieth Century,* with catalogue essays by Strauss; and *Between Dog & Wolf: Essays on Art & Politics* He received a Guggenheim fellowship to write his next book, *Photography & Belief.* Strauss teaches in the Graduate School of the Arts and at the Center for Curatorial Studies at Bard College.

Brooke Warner is a freelance writer and fulltime editor at North Atlantic Books. A graduate of The George Washington University, Warner has a degree in International Affairs and has traveled extensively, including to the Middle East and Southeast Asia. She is the co-editor of *Panic: Origins, Insight, and Treatment,* published by North Atlantic Books in 2002. Warner lives in the Bay Area.